# Standing as a Living Man or Woman in Canada: Reclaiming Freedom Beyond Statutes and Policy

Roger Davies

Published by TWON Publications, 2025.

STANDING AS A LIVING MAN OR WOMAN IN CANADA: RECLAIMING FREEDOM BEYOND STATUTES AND POLICY

**First edition. September 23, 2025.**



ISBN: 979-8231611546

Written by Roger Davies.

# Table of Contents

## Dedication

This book is dedicated to all Sovereign men and women of Canada who choose to live in honour, speak truth when others remain silent, and guard their freedom even when the cost is high. Your courage lights the way for generations to come.

## Disclaimer

This work presents ideas held by Sovereign men and women. It is intended for education and discussion. It is not legal advice, and no part of it replaces personal responsibility. Each reader must stand in their own truth and act according to their own conscience.

*"No law is above truth, and no statute can erase the birthright of a living man or woman. Freedom is not granted. It is lived."*

# Introduction

Freedom is not granted by governments, legislatures, or courts. It is not printed in an Act, nor is it bestowed by any Charter. Freedom is born with you. It flows from life itself, inseparable from breath and spirit. Every man and woman knows this truth deep within. Yet in modern Canada, few live it. From birth to death, Canadians are bound by documents, codes, licences, and demands that were never openly agreed to. They are trained to accept government as master and themselves as subject. This book exists to show another way.

To understand what has been done to Canadians, you must begin with the fact that two versions of you exist. One is the living man or woman, flesh and blood, capable of thought, honour, and choice. The other is a paper creation, built through registration, capital letters, and accounts. This second version is the Strawman. It looks like you, sounds like you, carries your name, but it is not you. It is a corporate fiction, a vessel for commerce, and the entry point for every demand from the state.

This is the silent trick. The Canadian government, its provinces, and all their agencies operate in commerce. They cannot touch the living soul directly, so they created a duplicate on paper. Through that duplicate, they claim ownership, taxation, and control. The result is that Canadians live under contracts they never knowingly signed. Every tax bill, every fine, every summons, every licence renewal is aimed at the Strawman. The living person steps forward, answers, and by doing so, creates joinder. That joinder is the hidden contract, the bridge that allows corporations to treat you as property.

Consider the birth certificate. It is presented to parents as proof of identity, a simple formality. Yet the act of registration is the creation of a legal entity. In law dictionaries and commercial codes, registration means transfer of ownership into a registry. From the moment of birth, the child is entered not only into a record of life but into a commercial system. That record becomes the anchor for bonds, financial instruments, and national obligations. The living child is reduced to an entry in an account. Every later demand, from taxes to licences, is built on that foundation.

In Canada, this system is wrapped in polite language. Officials speak of rights, benefits, and protections. Citizens are told that taxes pay for hospitals and schools. Courts are described as houses of justice. Police are shown as protectors of safety. Licences are sold as safeguards. Yet at the core, each of these is a contract, offered in silence and enforced by presumption. The government presumes you consented. Unless you rebut, the presumption stands. This is the quiet fraud that enslaves millions without chains or shackles.

Look at taxation. The Canada Revenue Agency presents itself as an authority, yet its demands are always addressed to the name in capitals. Its notices are crafted as offers that appear mandatory. Canadians are trained to believe income tax is law, when in reality it is a commercial obligation based on consent. You consent when you declare yourself a taxpayer, when you sign returns, when you apply for a Social Insurance Number. Without those steps, there is no contract. The illusion of duty is maintained through fear and repetition, not lawful obligation.

Courts in Canada operate under the same deception. The crest, the robes, the elevated bench, all are designed to impress upon the mind that justice is taking place. But the first act of any court is to call the name. If you stand and answer, you accept that you are the Strawman. At that moment, jurisdiction is created. The case moves forward not as truth but as commerce. The judge is not acting as a servant of natural law, but as an administrator of contracts. He balances ledgers, not justice.

The police, including the Royal Canadian Mounted Police and provincial services, reveal this structure clearly. They are not peace officers upholding natural law. They are policy enforcers. Their very name reveals it. "Police" comes from "policy." They enforce statutes and codes, not truth. When they stop you on the road, they are not protecting safety but enforcing conditions of a licence. When they issue tickets, they are creating invoices against the Strawman. When they demand identification, they are seeking joinder. The moment you comply, you contract.

The Charter of Rights and Freedoms is another illusion. It is presented as a safeguard, proof that Canada is free. Yet read its words carefully. Every right is subject to "reasonable limits prescribed by law." A right that can be limited by statute is not a right at all, but a privilege. The Charter does not create freedom. It creates permissions that can be withdrawn. True freedom exists before and beyond the Charter. It comes from being a living man or woman, not from a page in a statute book.

Education and media in Canada ensure this system continues. From an early age, children are taught to respect authority, obey rules, and accept citizenship as a badge of honour. They are never told about the Strawman. They are never told that licences and taxes are contracts. Instead, they are filled with stories of duty and pride. Television and newspapers ridicule anyone who challenges the system, branding them extremists or cranks. Fear of ridicule keeps most people silent. The few who question are drowned out by repetition and scorn.

Banks and debt are central to the trap. In Canada, as elsewhere, banks create money out of nothing using only signatures. A mortgage, loan, or credit card is not a gift of wealth from a bank, but an illusion of credit created by the borrower's promise. Yet the courts and police enforce these debts as if they were real. Families lose homes, men and women work lifetimes to repay numbers typed into accounts. This is not commerce in truth but servitude through deception.

The goal of this book is to reveal these structures as they exist in Canada. Each chapter will focus on one area: the birth certificate, taxation, licences, courts, police, banks, education, media, and more. You will see how each system relies not on force but on presumption. You will see how consent is tricked, not given. You will learn how men and women in Canada have stood as living beings, refusing joinder, issuing notices, and holding to honour. Their victories, though rarely reported, prove that the system is weaker than it appears.

This is not about rebellion, violence, or chaos. It is about knowledge, peace, and honour. The living man or woman does not need to fight, for he already holds freedom. The task is to remember it and to stand firm when asked to surrender it. The system thrives on silence, fear, and ignorance. It crumbles when faced with knowledge and calm resistance.

Ask yourself some questions. Did you ever knowingly sign a contract giving the Government of Canada authority over your life. Did you ever agree to be property of a Crown corporation. Did you ever consent to being treated as a legal fiction rather than a living soul. The answer is always no. The only way the system survives is by presuming consent where none exists. By standing in truth, by withdrawing consent, by refusing to act as the Strawman, you reclaim what was always yours.

Throughout this book, maxims of law will be presented. These are timeless principles: consent makes law, he who fails to deny agrees, the burden of proof rests on the claimant, no one is obliged to accept a benefit. These are the weapons of the free man and woman. They require no violence, no rebellion, only clarity and courage. When used with honour, they are stronger than any statute.

Canada is a land rich with natural beauty and resources. Its people are generous and resilient. Yet the corporate state has turned that wealth into a cage. It taxes, regulates, licences, and polices every act, while hiding behind polite language of democracy and rights. The living man or woman need not accept this. The cage is built on paper. Paper burns in the light of truth.

The chapters ahead will not give you freedom, for you already have it. They will show you the illusions that keep you from living it. They will show you how to walk in honour, how to speak with clarity, how to use notices and affidavits to rebut presumption. They will show you the victories of Canadians who stood firm, and they will encourage you to do the same.

You are not a citizen. You are not a resident. You are not a taxpayer. You are not a debtor. You are a living man or woman. You were born free, and nothing in law can alter that. The system depends on you forgetting. This book is here to help you remember.

The path of sovereignty in Canada is not easy. It requires courage, patience, and honour. But it is the only path that respects your birthright. As you read, keep one truth in your heart: you are not property of the state. You are not a corporate entry. You are life itself, free by birth and bound by no contract you did not knowingly sign. The system falls the moment you refuse to stand as the Strawman.

This is the beginning.

# Chapter 1: The Creation of the Strawman in Canada

The first chain is fastened at birth. A child enters the world as a living being, yet within days, that sacred life is captured on paper. Parents are told to register the birth. They are told it is compulsory, that it secures identity, health care, and education. Few stop to ask what registration means. In law, to register is to transfer ownership into a registry. The act that seems harmless is in truth a contract. The living child is recorded not as a sovereign being but as a corporate entity. That entity is the Strawman.

The Strawman is not spoken of in schools or media, yet it is central to how every Canadian is controlled. It is the legal fiction that stands between you and the state. It is written in capital letters, tied to numbers, and recognised only as a corporate vessel. You can see its presence in every document issued by government: passports, licences, tax bills, and summonses. They are never addressed to you, the living man or woman. They are always addressed to the Strawman. By responding, you accept the role and create joinder.

The use of capital letters is no accident. In commercial law, ships, corporations, and trusts are recorded in capitals. When you receive a letter that shouts your name in capitals, it is not speaking to your living self. It is speaking to a corporate construct. The trick works because no one ever explains it. Parents do not question it, schools do not teach it, and officials never admit it. Yet the effect is profound. A paper identity is formed, and all contracts, taxes, and fines attach to that identity.

Think about the first years of life. To enrol a child in school, parents must present the birth certificate. To apply for a health card, the same certificate is required. To open a bank account or apply for a passport, the certificate is the anchor. At every turn, the system demands proof not of the living being but of the registered entity. Canadians grow up believing that they exist only through paper. The truth is inverted. The living child breathes, thinks, and feels without documents. The Strawman is lifeless, yet it is treated as the only recognised person in commerce.

This arrangement is not unique to Canada, but Canada has refined it through its close ties to Crown corporations and international registries. The province records the birth, the federal government issues the Social Insurance Number, and together these create a commercial account. Researchers point to CUSIP numbers and international bonds tied to these registrations. Whether or not each claim is proven, the pattern is clear. The birth certificate is not simply a record of life. It is the foundation of a financial system that treats every Canadian as collateral.

The consequences appear when you encounter authority. A police officer asks for your name and date of birth. A government form requires your signature. A court calls your name in capitals. These acts are invitations to stand as the Strawman. The moment you comply, jurisdiction is established. The officer, the bureaucrat, and the judge are no longer dealing with a free man or woman. They are dealing with a corporate entity bound by contracts. Consent is assumed. Silence is taken as agreement. The living soul disappears behind the mask of the Strawman.

History shows how different life once was. Births were recorded in family Bibles, church books, or by the memory of kin. Communities recognised children without reference to central registries. Honour, duty, and custom shaped responsibility. The state intruded slowly, first offering convenience, then demanding compliance. By the twentieth century, registration had become normal. Parents were told it was compulsory. They were not told they were creating a legal person separate from the child. That silence hides the true purpose.

The moment of registration is carefully chosen. Parents are emotional, exhausted, and vulnerable. They want to do what is right for their child. Officials present forms with authority. The tone is firm. The message is that services and protections depend on registration. Few parents are in a state to question terms. They sign. With that signature, a new entity is created. From then on, the state has a foothold in the life of the family. The Strawman becomes the target of every future demand.

Look at how the system repeats the pattern. To drive, you must present the birth certificate. To marry, the same. To apply for employment, again. Each step strengthens the link between the living person and the Strawman. The more you comply, the deeper the assumption that you are one and the same. By adulthood, most Canadians have accepted dozens of contracts tied to the Strawman without realising it. Their lives are governed not by natural law but by commercial obligations disguised as statutes.

Consider the Social Insurance Number. It is sold as necessary for work and pensions. In truth, it is an account number in a fiscal scheme. Every wage, tax, and benefit is tied to that number. It is not assigned to the living being but to the registered entity. When you use it, you step into the role of taxpayer, a role created entirely through the Strawman. Without the Strawman, there is no duty. With it, obligations multiply endlessly.

This system thrives on presumption. The state does not prove you are the Strawman. It assumes you are, unless you say otherwise. It does not prove you owe tax. It assumes you do, unless you rebut. It does not prove you consented to jurisdiction. It assumes you did, unless you withhold consent. Every interaction rests on this fragile foundation. The moment you see it, the spell begins to break.

Canadians who have recognised the Strawman often report small victories. A man who received a council tax demand asked whether it was addressed to the registered entity or the living man. The office failed to reply and the demand was dropped. A woman faced with a traffic ticket asked for proof of contract between her and the province. None could be shown. The case faded away. These stories are rarely shared in mainstream media, but they circulate in private circles. They prove that the Strawman is the weak link in the chain.

The system relies on fear and ridicule to protect the illusion. Those who question birth registration or Strawman theory are mocked as conspiracy theorists. Television portrays them as extremists. Newspapers dismiss them without consideration. This ridicule is not accidental. It is a defence mechanism. If too many Canadians understood the trick, the entire system would collapse. Fear of ridicule is used to silence inquiry, and most accept the mockery rather than risk standing in truth.

Yet courage changes everything. A simple question asked calmly can unravel presumption. Who is being addressed. Where is the contract. What proof exists that I consented. These are not arguments or refusals. They are requests for clarity. When no proof is offered, the claim falls. Honour is preserved, and freedom remains intact.

The deeper lesson is that the Strawman exists only on paper. It has no life, no soul, no spirit. It cannot breathe, think, or act. It is a commercial convenience for governments and corporations. The living man or woman is always greater. The system cannot compel a free soul without consent. It can only invite, deceive, and presume. Once you stop playing the role, its power evaporates.

Think of the symbolism. A child is born into the world, perfect and free. Within days, a piece of paper is created to represent that child. That paper becomes the focus of life. It is used for schools, jobs, licences, taxes, courts, and debts. The living being is overshadowed by a lifeless duplicate. Society trains the child to believe that he is the paper. He grows up serving the Strawman, never realising that he was sovereign all along.

The question you must ask yourself is simple. When did you agree to be property of a corporation. When did you consent to be treated as a vessel in commerce. When did you sign a contract handing your sovereignty to a registry. The answer is clear. You never did. The signature on the birth record was not yours. The agreements that followed were given without full knowledge. Consent was assumed, never granted. That is the fraud at the heart of the Strawman.

The Strawman is a shadow, yet it casts a long influence over every Canadian life. Once you see the trick, the question becomes how to live without feeding it. To answer, you must first trace how the system expands the fiction into every area of existence. At birth, the certificate is issued. Next, the Social Insurance Number is applied for. Later, a driver's licence, a health card, a marriage licence, and a passport are added. Each new document does not recognise the living soul. It strengthens the paper construct. In time, the Strawman becomes a cage, enclosing the man or woman who unknowingly wears its mask.

The health system in Canada shows the reach of the Strawman clearly. Access to hospitals and doctors is tied to a health card, which in turn is tied to the registered entity. People are told that health care is a right of citizenship, yet in truth it is an administrative benefit granted through the Strawman. Without the paper identity, there is no access. The living body, though the very subject of health, is ignored. This contradiction shows the absurdity of the system. A body that bleeds, breathes, and suffers is treated as invisible, while a card of plastic determines whether help is given.

Employment follows the same path. Employers demand a Social Insurance Number before offering work. That number links wages to the Strawman, not to the living man or woman. Taxes, deductions, and pension contributions are all applied against the account. Without the number, most employers refuse to hire. Again, the paper fiction takes priority over the living soul. Canadians believe they are working for their families, yet in reality they are working for the maintenance of a corporate account. The Strawman is fed while the man or woman grows weary.

The passport extends this deception across borders. A Canadian who wishes to travel is told he must carry a passport. That document is not proof of life but proof of registration. It identifies the bearer as a citizen, which means a subject of the Crown. Every border crossing confirms the jurisdiction of the corporate state. Without the passport, travel is restricted. With it, the individual consents to be treated as property of Canada. The living man or woman is forgotten in the shuffle of queues and customs desks.

Marriage, too, is pulled into the registry. A union between man and woman is a natural act requiring no permission. Yet the state demands a licence. By applying, the couple turns their private bond into a corporate relationship. Children born of the marriage are tied even more tightly to the registry. The Strawman is expanded to encompass family life. What was sacred and private becomes subject to corporate oversight. The cycle of registration continues, generation after generation, without pause.

The courts provide the clearest view of the Strawman's power. When summoned, the first words spoken are the name in capitals. The judge, the clerk, and the bailiff wait for response. If the man or woman answers, jurisdiction is established. If silence is maintained or the question is returned, confusion arises. The court depends entirely on the presumption that the accused or claimant is the Strawman. Without that, the system struggles. Canadians who have refused to answer to the name have seen cases collapse or be abandoned. Though rare, such moments reveal the fragility of the illusion.

Police encounters work the same way. An officer asks, "What is your name?" By replying, you give life to the Strawman. The officer writes the name in capitals on a ticket or report. That document is then processed as if it binds the living being. The officer never asks for proof of contract, nor does he establish jurisdiction openly. He relies on consent given through compliance. When you hand over a licence, when you confirm an address, you are not acting as a free man or woman. You are stepping into the role of corporate entity.

Debt is another web spun from the Strawman. A bank loan is not created from money held in reserves. It is created by your signature, yet enforced against the Strawman. The bank treats the signature as an asset, then issues credit from nothing. The debt is collected through courts and agencies, all aimed at the registered entity. The living being provided the energy, the promise, yet is trapped by a paper fiction. Canadians work lifetimes to repay numbers typed into screens. The Strawman becomes the debtor, and the man or woman pays the price.

Consider the language of government. Citizens are addressed in all communications. Benefits, rights, and obligations are written to apply to citizens, residents, or taxpayers. None of these words describe the living man or woman. They describe corporate roles tied to the Strawman. To be a citizen is to be a member of a corporation. To be a taxpayer is to accept liability under a commercial contract. To be a resident is to hold a status created by statute. Each is a mask, not reality. The living man or woman is none of these. Yet by failing to rebut, most Canadians accept the masks.

Education plays a central role in this deception. From kindergarten onward, children are taught to memorise their name, Social Insurance Number, and date of birth. They are tested on citizenship, rights, and duties. They are never told that these are corporate constructs. Instead, they are encouraged to take pride in being good citizens. Loyalty to the state is presented as virtue. The Strawman is fed while the child is conditioned to forget natural sovereignty. By adulthood, the deception is complete. The individual believes that paper is more real than life.

Media enforces the same message. Those who question the Strawman are mocked as radicals. News anchors use words like "sovereign citizen" as insults. Courts are portrayed as bastions of justice. Police are shown as noble protectors. Taxes are described as the price of civilisation. Licences are praised as safeguards. These messages repeat endlessly until most people stop asking questions. Yet beneath the noise, the truth remains. The Strawman is a fiction. Its power comes only from belief. Without belief, it collapses.

What happens when a Canadian refuses the role of Strawman. Stories circulate of men and women who have stood firm. A farmer who refused to answer to his name in court saw the judge dismiss the case. A mother who demanded proof of contract from a provincial agency received no reply, and the matter was dropped. A driver who asked whether the licence was a contract withdrew consent, and the ticket vanished. These accounts are not reported in mainstream outlets, yet they show what is possible. The system is strong only against the uninformed. Against knowledge and honour, it falters.

The maxims of law remind us why. He who leaves silent is taken to agree. Consent makes law. No one is obliged to accept a benefit. These principles are older than Canada, older than the Crown, older than any statute. They are universal truths. The Strawman system survives only by twisting them. It assumes consent through silence. It treats benefits as obligations. It disguises contracts as laws. By invoking the maxims, a man or woman restores balance. The presumption falls, and the truth stands.

The deeper you look, the clearer it becomes. Every demand from the state is directed not to the living soul but to the Strawman. Every signature strengthens the bond. Every answer to the name confirms the fiction. The escape is simple, though not always easy. Do not consent. Do not act as the Strawman. Speak as the living man or woman. Demand proof of contract. Place your notices on the record. Stand in honour. The system has no answer to this.

The creation of the Strawman in Canada is the foundation of all other controls. Without it, taxes could not be collected, licences could not be enforced, and courts could not claim jurisdiction. With it, every man and woman is trapped in a web of presumed obligations. That is why this chapter comes first. Until you see the birth of the fiction, you cannot understand the rest of the system. Once you see it, the pieces fall into place.

The Strawman is a mask. You were not born with it. It was placed on you by registry. You are free to remove it. The state will resist, banks will protest, courts will mock, but they cannot deny the truth. You are a living man or woman, and no piece of paper can alter that. The task ahead is to remember, to speak, and to live accordingly. That is the first step on the path of sovereignty in Canada.

# Chapter 2: The Crown Corporation

Canada presents itself to the world as a sovereign nation, free and democratic, founded on the rule of law. Schoolbooks tell children that Canada became independent in 1867, that its Parliament governs for the people, and that its institutions serve the public good. Yet beneath the flag and anthem lies a very different structure. Canada is not the free country most imagine. It is a corporate entity, bound to the Crown, registered in commerce, and operating through statutes and contracts.

To see this truth, you must look at the language of government itself. The Government of Canada describes itself as "Her Majesty the Queen in Right of Canada." Provinces describe themselves as "Her Majesty the Queen in Right of Ontario," or "in Right of British Columbia." This phrase is not poetic. It is legal. It shows that Canada and its provinces are not independent entities. They exist as Crown corporations. The Queen—or now the King—holds ultimate title, and the governments act as corporate branches under that authority.

Every Canadian has seen the evidence without recognising it. Court documents, Acts of Parliament, and provincial statutes all open with references to the Crown. Police officers swear oaths to the Crown, not to the people. Judges wear robes marked with Crown symbols. Coins and banknotes bear the face of the monarch. These are not decorations. They are reminders that Canada is a possession of the Crown, managed as a corporation.

In commerce, corporations are legal fictions. They exist only on paper, created through registration. A government that calls itself "Her Majesty in Right of Canada" is admitting that it is a corporate fiction. It has no life of its own. It functions through officers, employees, and contracts. This explains why every interaction with the state is handled through paperwork. Applications, licences, fines, and taxes are processed not as matters of living law but as matters of corporate policy. Canadians believe they are dealing with a government of the people, but in truth they are dealing with a company.

Look at how Canada interacts internationally. It is listed in commercial registries such as Dun & Bradstreet. It signs treaties not as a nation of free people but as a contracting party. Its revenue comes from taxation, fees, and debt—all classic features of a corporation. Like any company, it balances budgets, borrows from banks, and pays interest. The people are not shareholders. They are treated as employees and debtors, providing labour and taxes to keep the corporation afloat.

The Crown itself is a complex structure. Canadians are taught that the monarchy is symbolic, a figurehead with no real power. Yet in law, the Crown is the owner of all land and resources. Every title deed in Canada acknowledges Crown ownership. Citizens are never true landowners. They are tenants, holding property in fee simple, which means on condition of service to the Crown. Taxes on land are rent payments. Failure to pay leads to eviction, proving the Crown's ultimate title. This is not freedom. It is tenancy under a landlord disguised as nationhood.

The connection between Crown and corporation is also revealed in courts. Cases are titled "Regina versus Smith" or "Rex versus Jones." The Crown is always the claimant. Whether the charge is theft, tax evasion, or traffic violation, the Crown is the party bringing the case. This shows that Canadian courts are not forums for justice between men and women. They are venues where the Crown corporation enforces its policies against corporate subjects. The individual is treated not as a sovereign being but as property of the Crown.

Even Parliament exposes the truth. Acts are passed "with the advice and consent of the Queen's Most Honourable Council." The language has not changed since colonial days. The illusion of democracy is maintained through elections, yet the structure remains corporate. Members of Parliament are employees of the corporation, bound by oath to the Crown. Their duty is not to the people but to the corporate entity they serve. This explains why governments consistently act against the interests of Canadians while claiming legal authority. They are serving their true master, not the living people.

The banking system completes the picture. The Bank of Canada is presented as a public institution, yet its operations are commercial. It issues currency as debt, lends to the government, and manages fiscal policy in partnership with international banks. Canadians assume their currency is national, yet it bears the image of the monarch and circulates as corporate notes. Every dollar in a Canadian's pocket is proof of subjection to the Crown corporation. It is not money of substance but credit issued by a corporate entity.

Think of how this affects daily life. A man buys land, believing he is a free owner. Yet every year he must pay property tax. If he fails, the municipality seizes the land. This proves the Crown owns the land, and the man is only a tenant. A woman works hard, earning wages. Income tax removes a portion automatically. She is told it is her duty as a citizen. In reality, she is paying rent to the Crown for the privilege of using a Strawman identity. The corporation feeds off her labour.

Even driving shows the corporate structure. The roads are said to be public, but they are registered to the Crown. To use them, a Canadian must apply for a licence. That licence is a contract with the Crown corporation. Every ticket issued is an invoice. Every fine collected is revenue. The police officer does not act as a peacekeeper. He acts as a revenue agent for the Crown. This is not the rule of law. It is the operation of a company maximising profit from its employees.

Media reinforces the illusion of independence. Canadians are told that the monarchy is symbolic, that Parliament governs, that courts uphold justice. Yet the symbols of the Crown appear everywhere. The corporate structure is hidden in plain sight. By dismissing questions as conspiracy and ridiculing those who raise them, the media protects the secret. The people remain compliant, believing they are free citizens when they are bound corporate subjects.

The corporate nature of Canada also explains its behaviour in crises. During emergencies, governments pass regulations by decree, citing Crown authority. Rights are suspended, businesses are closed, and movement is restricted. These acts are not democratic. They are corporate policies imposed on employees. The people comply because they believe the corporation is their government. In truth, they are consenting to corporate management.

The pattern is consistent across all provinces and territories. Each identifies itself as "Her Majesty the Queen in Right of..." followed by the province name. Each operates through ministries, departments, and agencies structured like corporate divisions. Each collects taxes and fees as revenue. Each holds land in the name of the Crown. Together, they form a corporate web that spans the entire country. The people are not represented. They are managed.

This reality changes how you view law in Canada. Statutes are not expressions of the people's will. They are corporate policies, binding only by consent. The Crown corporation has no natural authority over living men and women. Its reach extends only through contracts and presumption. This is why notices and affidavits can be effective. By rebutting presumption, by refusing joinder, you step outside the corporate structure. The Crown has no lawful power to compel a sovereign being.

Canadians who understand this have begun to live differently. Some refuse licences, choosing to travel as free men and women. Others challenge taxes, demanding proof of contract. Some place notices on the record, declaring they are not corporate entities. These acts are met with resistance, ridicule, and sometimes force. Yet they reveal cracks in the system. The Crown corporation depends on ignorance. Knowledge weakens it. Honour destroys it.

The truth of Canada's corporate nature is revealed most clearly when you follow the money. Corporations exist to generate revenue, and Canada is no different. Its revenue streams come from taxation, fines, licences, and borrowing. Every interaction with the state results in payment. You are told these payments fund services, yet the bulk of revenue goes to interest on debt and the maintenance of the corporate system itself. Hospitals close, schools crumble, but interest payments continue without fail. This shows where loyalty lies. The Crown corporation serves its creditors, not its people.

Debt is the lifeblood of the corporation. Canada borrows billions each year, not from its citizens but from international banks and investors. These loans are secured against the labour and assets of Canadians, treated as collateral. Each birth certificate represents future productivity pledged to the lenders. The people are not asked for consent. They are simply enrolled as debt slaves from birth. Generations work not to build their own wealth but to service obligations contracted by corporate officers in Ottawa. This is not sovereignty. It is servitude under commercial law.

The way Canada treats its natural resources also reveals the corporate model. Oil, timber, minerals, and water are extracted under Crown licence. Companies pay royalties to the Crown, not to the people. The revenue disappears into corporate coffers, while communities are left with pollution and poverty. If Canada were truly a nation of free people, resources would belong to the people collectively. Instead, they belong to the Crown, managed for profit like assets of a company. Canadians are tenants on their own land, allowed to survive but never to truly own.

Even the national flag can be understood in corporate terms. Before 1965, Canada flew the Red Ensign, which bore direct reference to the Crown. The Maple Leaf flag was introduced as a corporate brand, a logo to mask the true ownership. Like a company redesigning its symbol to refresh its image, Canada rebranded itself while leaving the structure untouched. Citizens were taught to salute the new flag with pride, never realising it marked them as employees of a Crown corporation.

The language of government budgets is corporate through and through. Ministers speak of deficits, surpluses, and fiscal responsibility. They describe taxpayers as the "revenue base." They present services as "deliverables." This is not the language of a sovereign nation. It is the language of a business. Citizens are not sovereign participants in law. They are customers, employees, and debtors. Their lives are managed through balance sheets, not principles.

The legal system mirrors this corporate mindset. Every statute is a policy manual. Every regulation is a corporate rule. The Criminal Code is not natural law but a collection of corporate policies designed to regulate employees. This explains why statutes are enforceable only against those who consent to be subjects. The living man or woman, standing outside the corporation, is not bound by internal policies. Only by stepping into the Strawman role does one fall under corporate rules. The law of the living remains unchanged: cause no harm, commit no fraud, honour your agreements.

International agreements confirm the corporate nature of Canada. Trade deals, treaties, and conventions are signed not by the people but by officers of the Crown. These agreements bind Canadians without their knowledge or consent. The corporation aligns itself with global partners, often against the interest of its employees. Farmers lose land, industries collapse, and jobs vanish, yet the corporation profits through international partnerships. Canadians bear the cost while the Crown expands its influence.

Military service provides another layer of evidence. The Canadian Forces swear loyalty to the Crown, not the people. Soldiers are trained to defend corporate interests abroad, often in conflicts that serve banking or resource agendas. They believe they fight for freedom, yet in truth they protect corporate profit. Veterans return broken and neglected, proof that the corporation values profit over people. If Canada were truly a free nation, its military would defend the people first. Instead, it defends the Crown and its creditors.

The taxation system is one of the clearest signs of corporate control. Income tax was introduced as a temporary measure during wartime but has become permanent. It is enforced not as natural duty but as corporate policy. The Canada Revenue Agency operates as a collection agency, issuing invoices disguised as tax assessments. Canadians comply because they fear penalties. Yet the agency never provides proof of contract. Its authority exists only through presumption. Without consent, its demands are empty. The corporation relies on fear and ignorance to maintain revenue flow.

Consider how corporations treat dissent. Whistle-blowers are silenced, employees who question policies are punished, and critics are marginalised. Canada behaves the same way. Those who expose corruption are prosecuted. Activists are surveilled. Journalists who dig too deeply lose access or employment. Citizens who challenge taxes or licences are ridiculed as extremists. This is not democratic debate. It is corporate discipline. The Crown corporation protects itself, not the truth.

The illusion of representation is maintained through elections. Canadians are told they choose their leaders. In reality, they choose between corporate managers, all sworn to the Crown. Policy does not change regardless of party. Taxes rise, debt grows, and freedoms shrink, no matter which colour of banner flies in Parliament. Elections are marketing exercises, designed to refresh public trust in the corporation. The structure remains untouched. The Crown continues to rule, and the people remain subjects.

This structure explains the frustration many Canadians feel. They see governments act against their interests, yet they are powerless to stop it. They sign petitions, march in protests, and cast ballots, but nothing changes. The reason is simple. They are not shareholders. They hold no stake in the corporation. They are employees bound by contract, without voting rights in the boardroom. Their voices are ignored because they are not recognised as sovereign beings. Only by stepping outside the corporation can they reclaim their true power.

The courts reveal this most brutally in foreclosure and eviction cases. A family misses mortgage payments, and the bank seizes the home with court approval. The judge rules in favour of the creditor because the debtor is treated as a corporate entity. The family believed they owned the land, but in truth they were tenants under Crown ownership. The bank enforces its contract, and the Crown enforces its title. The family is left on the street, while the corporation profits. This is not justice. It is commerce.

The education system ensures this cycle continues. Students are taught national pride, loyalty to the Charter, and the importance of paying taxes. They are not taught the truth of the Crown corporation. They are conditioned to serve as employees, consumers, and debtors. By the time they reach adulthood, they have internalised the corporate identity. They believe citizenship is an honour when it is a chain. They accept taxation as duty when it is theft. They obey statutes as law when they are policies. The corporation thrives on their ignorance.

Breaking free begins with recognition. Once you see Canada as a corporation, the pieces align. The birth certificate becomes the entry point, the Social Insurance Number becomes the account number, and taxation becomes the invoice system. Courts, police, and banks all operate as departments of the corporation. The monarch remains the owner, and the people remain tenants. Knowing this truth strips away the illusion of democracy and reveals the cage for what it is.

The remedy lies in standing as the living man or woman. Corporations cannot command life. They can only contract with other corporations. By refusing joinder, by rejecting the Strawman, you step beyond corporate reach. Notices and affidavits become powerful tools because they expose the presumption. They remind officers that you are not property of the Crown. You are not an employee of a corporation. You are a free man or woman.

This path is not without challenge. The Crown corporation defends itself fiercely. It uses police to intimidate, courts to punish, and media to ridicule. But its power is fragile. It rests entirely on consent. The moment you withdraw consent, its foundation crumbles. A corporation without employees cannot function. A government without subjects cannot rule. The Crown survives only because Canadians forget they are sovereign. Remembering changes everything.

The Crown corporation is the greatest illusion in Canadian life. It presents itself as nation, democracy, and protector, yet it is none of these. It is a business, extracting revenue from employees while serving international creditors. It owns the land, controls the courts, manages the police, and enslaves the people through paperwork. Its strength lies in deception. Its weakness lies in truth. Once you see it, you are free. The task ahead is to live that freedom, to stand outside the corporation, and to remind others that they too are sovereign.

# Chapter 3: The Charter Illusion

Canadians are told they are blessed with one of the most advanced charters of rights in the world. Teachers repeat it, judges cite it, and politicians wave it as proof of freedom. The Canadian Charter of Rights and Freedoms is praised as the crown jewel of democracy. It hangs on classroom walls, is quoted in courtrooms, and is used to silence dissent. Yet behind the glittering language lies an uncomfortable truth. The Charter does not secure freedom. It limits it. It does not recognise sovereignty. It replaces it with conditional privileges.

To understand this, look closely at the text itself. Section 1 declares that the rights and freedoms set out in the Charter are "subject to such reasonable limits prescribed by law as can be demonstrably justified in a free and democratic society." These words destroy the illusion at once. A right that is subject to limits is not a right. It is a permission. True rights cannot be taken away. They exist by virtue of being alive. When a document says your rights may be restricted by statute, it is admitting those rights are privileges. The Charter, far from protecting Canadians, places them under Crown control.

Consider freedom of expression. Canadians are told they can speak their minds. Yet hate speech laws, human rights codes, and defamation statutes all place boundaries around speech. The Charter does not forbid these boundaries. It allows them. When a journalist is silenced, or a citizen fined for words, courts declare the restriction a "reasonable limit." The result is that freedom of expression in Canada exists only within boundaries set by the state. That is not freedom. It is controlled permission.

The same applies to mobility rights. The Charter promises Canadians the ability to move freely within the country. Yet restrictions are easily imposed. Provinces can set health rules, border checks, or licensing conditions. The federal government can ban travel through regulations. During emergencies, mobility can be restricted entirely. Courts uphold these restrictions as "reasonable." Again, the supposed right is revealed as fragile. The living man or woman is free to travel by birth, yet under the Charter, travel is a licensed activity subject to corporate policy.

Property rights are another example. Canadians often assume the Charter protects private ownership. It does not. There is no guaranteed property right in the Charter. Land remains under Crown title, and ownership exists only in fee simple. Governments can seize property for taxes, expropriate land for projects, or restrict use through zoning. The Charter provides no defence. This silence is not accidental. It reflects the corporate reality of Canada. The people are tenants, not owners. The Charter hides this fact by never acknowledging property as a natural right.

The Charter also places all rights beneath the Crown. Section 32 specifies that the Charter applies only to Parliament and provincial legislatures, not to private corporations or individuals. This means that the Charter is not a universal declaration of freedom. It is an internal policy manual for government bodies. It binds only those acting on behalf of the Crown. For the living man or woman, it offers no shield. When banks, employers, or agencies act against you, the Charter often has nothing to say. Canadians are shocked to discover this, yet it is written plainly in the text.

The very name of the Charter reveals the deception. A charter, in law, is a grant from a sovereign to subjects. It is not a recognition of inherent freedom. It is a gift, revocable at will. Medieval kings issued charters to towns, allowing them to hold markets or govern themselves. Those rights could be withdrawn at any time. The Canadian Charter of Rights and Freedoms follows the same pattern. It is not a declaration that Canadians are free. It is a corporate licence, granting privileges while reserving ultimate authority to the Crown.

This becomes clear in times of crisis. When the government declares an emergency, rights vanish. Curfews are imposed, businesses are closed, gatherings are banned, and speech is restricted. Courts uphold these measures as reasonable. The Charter is powerless to stop them, because it was never designed to protect sovereignty. It was designed to regulate subjects. The living man or woman remains free, but those acting as Strawmen are bound by the corporation's rules. Canadians who rely on the Charter for protection are repeatedly disappointed.

The Charter is often compared to the American Bill of Rights, yet the difference is profound. The Bill of Rights recognises rights as existing prior to government. It says "Congress shall make no law" restricting them. The Canadian Charter, by contrast, says rights are subject to limits. It grants, then withdraws. It offers, then conditions. Canadians believe they are equal to Americans in freedom, yet in truth they live under a corporate charter, not a declaration of natural rights.

The Charter also creates a culture of dependency. Citizens are taught to beg courts for their rights. Lawyers argue cases, judges interpret clauses, and governments claim authority to balance freedom against policy. The result is that Canadians see rights as gifts from the state rather than inherent qualities of life. This mentality weakens sovereignty. A free man or woman does not ask permission to speak, travel, or live. They act in honour and refuse harm. The Charter turns natural freedom into corporate bargaining.

Consider the case of expression during political protests. Canadians have marched against taxes, lockdowns, and government policies. Many were arrested, fined, or silenced. They appealed to the Charter, only to be told their freedoms were subject to "reasonable limits." Judges sided with the Crown, declaring restrictions necessary. The protesters discovered that the Charter was not their shield but their cage. It defined the boundaries of dissent and legitimised punishment beyond them.

Education again plays its role. Children are taught to revere the Charter as the source of their rights. Teachers explain that without it, Canadians would have no freedom. This is the opposite of truth. Rights existed long before the Charter. The Charter did not create them. It redefined them as privileges. By teaching children to depend on a corporate document, schools ensure that future generations never question the system. Pride in the Charter becomes pride in servitude.

The illusion is further strengthened by media. Journalists praise the Charter, citing it as proof of Canadian decency. When government restricts freedom, media outlets explain it away with the language of reasonableness. Rarely do they admit that a right so easily limited is no right at all. Those who question the Charter's legitimacy are mocked as radicals. The illusion is preserved by repetition. Canadians hear so often that the Charter guarantees freedom that they stop reading its words.

Yet when you read, the truth is undeniable. Every right is conditional. Every clause is subject to statute. Nowhere does the Charter acknowledge the sovereignty of the living man or woman. It speaks only to citizens, subjects, and residents. It assumes the corporate framework created by the Strawman. The free soul is invisible in its pages.

For those seeking sovereignty, the Charter is not a remedy. It is a trap. Invoking it in court is to step into the corporate arena, accepting the rules of the game. Sovereign men and women do not beg for rights from a charter. They assert their freedoms as birthrights, beyond statute, beyond government, beyond Crown. The Charter may appear as shield, but it is made of paper. It burns in the fire of truth.

The Charter is often waved like a banner by politicians who claim to defend freedom. Yet when you examine their actions, you see the contradiction. They praise the Charter while passing laws that erode liberty. They swear oaths to the Crown, not to the people, then tell Canadians the Charter protects them. In reality, the Charter is their shield against accountability. They argue that every restriction is permitted because it is "reasonable." The more power they claim, the more they point to the Charter as justification. It is not a restraint. It is a licence to govern without limits.

Canadians have watched as courts upheld restrictions on gatherings, speech, and movement. Each time, judges explained that the Charter allows such limits. Citizens expected protection but received excuses. The Charter was not designed to stop government. It was designed to manage dissent. By giving the illusion of rights, it pacifies the population. By allowing endless exceptions, it guarantees government authority. This is why officials speak so confidently of the Charter. They know it secures their power, not your freedom.

The absence of property rights is one of the most telling features. No government document that claims to protect rights omits ownership by accident. Land is the foundation of independence. A man who owns his land can feed his family, shelter himself, and resist control. A man who holds only title from the Crown is dependent. Canada deliberately excludes property rights to keep its subjects in dependence. Taxes, zoning laws, and expropriation become tools of control. The Charter remains silent because it was never written to empower the people. It was written to empower the corporation.

The Charter also divides freedom into categories, giving the illusion of variety while ensuring control. It lists freedoms of conscience, religion, expression, assembly, and association. Yet each is paired with exceptions. Freedom of religion is limited by human rights codes. Freedom of assembly is limited by permits. Freedom of association is limited by labour laws. The corporate state dangles rights like carrots, then yanks them away when inconvenient. Citizens are left chasing illusions, believing they have choices while remaining bound.

The role of the judiciary is central to maintaining the illusion. Judges claim to interpret the Charter, but their interpretations always favour the Crown. When citizens argue for broader freedoms, judges rule against them. When governments argue for more power, judges rule in their favour. This is not impartiality. It is corporate loyalty. Judges are officers of the Crown, sworn to uphold the corporate structure. Their robes and symbols reflect this allegiance. To expect them to defend sovereignty is to expect a servant to betray his master.

Lawyers contribute to the trap. They train for years in the language of the Charter, billing clients thousands to argue cases within its framework. They rarely question the legitimacy of the framework itself. They teach clients to beg for privileges instead of asserting rights. By doing so, they ensure dependence on the legal system. Sovereign men and women who represent themselves often expose the limits of the Charter more clearly than lawyers ever will. They refuse to play the corporate game, demanding proof of contract rather than appealing to paper privileges.

Education has drilled into generations of Canadians that the Charter is sacred. Children memorise its clauses, teachers celebrate its anniversaries, and media produce glowing tributes. Little attention is paid to its weaknesses. Few are told about Section 1, the clause that strips all rights of permanence. Fewer still are told about the absence of property rights. Most Canadians grow up believing the Charter makes them free. In reality, it makes them obedient. Pride in the Charter becomes pride in chains.

The Charter's defenders argue that it balances freedom with order. They say absolute rights would be dangerous, that limits are necessary. But freedom with limits is not freedom. It is controlled behaviour. The natural law requires only that one cause no harm, commit no fraud, and honour agreements. Beyond this, no man has authority over another. The Charter rejects this simplicity. It replaces natural law with corporate statutes, all dressed up as reasonable limits. Canadians are trained to accept this as justice, when it is nothing more than commercial management.

Look at recent history. During times of national crisis, governments have restricted gatherings, closed businesses, and silenced critics. Citizens appealed to the Charter. Courts replied that restrictions were justified. The result was mass compliance. Canadians accepted the closure of churches, the arrest of protesters, and the censorship of speech because they believed the Charter still protected them. In truth, the Charter had already authorised their subjugation. Its words gave governments the power they claimed to restrain.

The illusion works because most Canadians never compare the Charter to natural freedom. They accept that freedom must come from paper. They accept that government defines its limits. They forget that freedom exists before law. A living man or woman does not need permission to speak, travel, or gather. These are natural expressions of life. The Charter teaches the opposite. It says you are free only when allowed. This reversal keeps Canadians in a permanent state of dependence.

Some Canadians have seen through the deception. They refuse to rely on the Charter in court, instead asserting their status as living men and women. They place notices on record declaring that their rights exist outside statute. They remind officials that rights cannot be granted or taken by government. These individuals are mocked, fined, or threatened, but their courage exposes the truth. By refusing the Charter, they refuse the cage. They remind the corporation that freedom cannot be licensed.

The Charter's true purpose is revealed in its history. It was introduced in 1982 as part of patriation, presented as a step toward full independence. In reality, it was a rebranding exercise. Canada remained under Crown authority, but citizens were given a shiny new document to believe in. The corporate structure did not change. The Strawman system remained intact. What changed was perception. Canadians were given a new story of freedom to mask the same servitude.

The language of Section 33, the "notwithstanding clause," makes this even clearer. It allows governments to override Charter rights entirely for five years at a time. What kind of right can be suspended by statute. A right that can be overridden is not a right. It is a privilege at the mercy of corporate officers. The presence of this clause proves that the Charter was never meant to secure liberty. It was meant to legitimise control.

The Charter illusion is powerful because it offers comfort. Citizens want to believe they are free. They want to believe their government protects them. The Charter provides that comfort, even as it chains them. It reassures while it restricts. It calms while it captures. To see through it is unsettling, but necessary. Without breaking the illusion, sovereignty cannot be reclaimed.

The path forward is not to abolish the Charter but to step beyond it. The living man or woman does not beg for rights under corporate documents. They assert freedom by birthright, governed only by natural law. They stand in honour, refuse joinder, and place notices on record. They do not argue clauses. They demand proof of contract. By living this way, they show others that the Charter is not the source of freedom but the mask of slavery.

Canadians who cling to the Charter will continue to be disappointed. Each time they test its limits, they will find the limits win. Each time they appeal to courts, they will find judges side with the Crown. The Charter will never deliver sovereignty, because it was never designed to. It was crafted to manage subjects, not to liberate them. Freedom lies outside its pages, in the simple truth that life itself is authority enough.

When you stop believing in the Charter, its power dissolves. It is a piece of paper, nothing more. It cannot breathe, think, or act. It cannot grant what you already possess. The true law is written in your being. You are born free, and no corporation, no Crown, no statute, and no charter can change that. The only question is whether you will live it.

# Chapter 4: Taxation by Consent

Taxation is presented to Canadians as a duty. From the first paycheque to the last pension deposit, citizens are told that paying tax is the price of civilisation. Politicians insist that taxes fund hospitals, schools, and roads. Media outlets repeat the message, portraying tax resistance as selfish and dangerous. The Canada Revenue Agency enforces compliance with threats of penalties, interest, and even prison. Yet few pause to ask a simple question: where is the proof of obligation. Where is the signed contract binding a living man or woman to pay income tax.

When you strip away propaganda, you find that taxation in Canada, like elsewhere, is built on consent. It is not law in the sense of natural duty. It is commerce. It is a system of offers, agreements, and presumed contracts. The state relies on paperwork, signatures, and silence to create obligations. Without consent, its power evaporates. This is why officials work so hard to disguise taxation as unavoidable law. They cannot admit that it depends entirely on the willingness of men and women to act as taxpayers.

The starting point is the Social Insurance Number. Canadians are told they must apply for a number to work legally. The application is voluntary, but once submitted it creates an account. That account identifies the applicant as a taxpayer. Wages are tied to it, deductions are calculated against it, and benefits are issued through it. The man or woman who never applied has no taxpayer account. Yet through social conditioning, nearly every Canadian applies without hesitation. Consent is secured, not by force, but by ignorance.

Consider the annual tax return. Each year, Canadians are instructed to file a return with the Canada Revenue Agency. The form requires a signature, affirming that the filer is a taxpayer and that the information is true. That signature is the binding act. Without it, there is no contract. The CRA cannot compel a living man or woman to sign. It can only invite. Yet millions comply, believing they have no choice. The consent is renewed annually, disguised as duty.

The language of the CRA itself reveals the truth. It calls people "taxpayers." It issues "notices of assessment." These are commercial terms. An assessment is an opinion of liability, not a fact. It is an offer to contract. By failing to rebut, the recipient is deemed to agree. Silence equals consent. This principle of commerce underpins the entire tax system. The government never proves obligation. It assumes it, and unless challenged, the assumption stands.

History provides context. Income tax in Canada began as a temporary measure during the First World War. It was sold as a patriotic duty, needed only for the duration of conflict. Yet once the system was in place, it never disappeared. Like any corporation that discovers a profitable revenue stream, the Crown maintained and expanded it. Over time, statutes were written, agencies were created, and propaganda was intensified. Canadians were trained to believe income tax was permanent and lawful. The truth—that it was always voluntary—was buried under generations of repetition.

Look at the mechanics of collection. Employers withhold tax from wages through payroll systems. This appears compulsory, but it is based on the employee's consent when providing a Social Insurance Number and signing employment forms. The employer acts as an agent of the CRA, but only because the worker agreed to the taxpayer role. Without that role, there is no lawful deduction. The system functions because nearly everyone consents at the start of employment, never questioning the contract.

The same principle applies to sales tax, property tax, and other levies. Sales tax is charged at the point of purchase, but only because the buyer uses the Strawman identity in commerce. Property tax is demanded annually, but only because ownership is held in fee simple under Crown title. In each case, the tax is not a universal law but a condition of a contract. By entering commerce as a citizen, resident, or taxpayer, Canadians accept the terms. The living man or woman, standing outside these roles, has no such obligations.

Examples of resistance exist, though rarely publicised. Some Canadians have refused to file returns, instead sending notices demanding proof of contract. Others have challenged assessments by asking for evidence that the CRA has lawful authority over living beings. In many cases, the agency fails to reply substantively. It threatens, intimidates, and sometimes seizes accounts, but it never produces a signed contract. This silence speaks volumes. The CRA knows its power rests on presumption. When the presumption is exposed, it has nothing to stand on.

The fear of punishment is the greatest weapon used to enforce compliance. Stories of audits, fines, and prison sentences are circulated widely. Media outlets highlight prosecutions of tax evaders, creating the impression that resistance is impossible. Yet closer inspection often reveals that those punished either admitted taxpayer status, signed returns, or engaged in fraudulent schemes. Rarely do you hear of a man or woman who simply refused consent, stood in honour, and demanded proof. Those cases are ignored because they would shatter the illusion of duty.

The moral argument for taxation is also weak. Politicians claim taxes fund public services, but billions are wasted on corporate bailouts, foreign wars, and interest payments on debt. Hospitals still charge fees, schools still demand fundraising, and roads remain in disrepair. The average Canadian sees little return on their taxes. The money flows upward, enriching banks and contractors, while ordinary families struggle. If taxation were truly about supporting society, the evidence would be visible. Instead, it is about maintaining the Crown corporation.

The principle of consent makes taxation easy to challenge. In commerce, the burden of proof rests on the claimant. If the CRA claims you owe, it must prove the obligation. If no contract exists, no debt exists. The agency relies on ignorance, hoping citizens will assume the burden themselves. But when asked for proof, it falters. The power lies not in fighting or evading, but in calmly demanding evidence. Where no contract is shown, no payment is due.

The illusion of obligation survives only because most Canadians never ask questions. They believe taxation is law because they were told so in school and reinforced through media. Yet if you look for the statute that compels a living man or woman to pay income tax, you will not find it. You will find acts and codes that apply to "taxpayers." You will find definitions of "persons," "residents," and "citizens." You will not find direct language binding the flesh-and-blood man or woman. The entire system relies on assumption, not truth.

Consider the way government correspondence is written. Letters from the CRA arrive with threatening language: "You must pay," "You are required," "Failure will result in penalties." Yet each is addressed to a name in capital letters. They never name the living being. They address the Strawman. If you answer without clarifying, you step into that role. The threats then appear to apply to you. But if you question who is being addressed, the agency struggles to respond. It knows it cannot lawfully bind you, so it relies on intimidation to draw you into contract.

The design of tax forms reveals the trick. They always require you to declare that you are a taxpayer. The signature confirms the role. Without that, the CRA cannot move forward. Even electronic filings require digital signatures that affirm taxpayer status. The contract is renewed every year. Millions sign without realising what they are agreeing to. They see it as duty, but in truth it is voluntary joinder with the corporate system.

This voluntary nature is why conditional acceptance is such a powerful tool. Instead of refusing outright, which can be misinterpreted as evasion, the sovereign man or woman accepts to pay on condition that proof of contract is provided. The CRA cannot meet the condition, because no contract exists. The offer collapses. Honour is maintained, because there is no refusal to pay a lawful debt. There is only a demand for evidence. This is the essence of standing as a living being in commerce: respond with honour, require proof, and expose presumption.

Examples of this approach are found across Canada. A man in Alberta responded to a tax demand with a notice of conditional acceptance, asking the CRA to show the signed agreement that made him a taxpayer. Months passed with no reply, and the matter was quietly dropped. A woman in Quebec challenged an assessment by filing an affidavit stating she was not the corporate entity named and had never signed a binding contract. The agency threatened, but never acted. Though not widely reported, these outcomes show that the system collapses when challenged in honour.

Fear of enforcement is the greatest obstacle. The CRA uses garnishment, liens, and seizures to frighten citizens. Yet these actions are aimed at bank accounts, wages, and property all tied to the Strawman. The living man or woman, who has placed notices on record and refused joinder, stands outside that reach. The agency cannot touch life. It can only seize paper assets. This is why notices of understanding and affidavits of truth are important. They create a record that you are not the corporate entity, removing the presumption before it can be used against you.

The idea that taxation is voluntary shocks most Canadians, yet the evidence is overwhelming. Every tax is linked to an act of consent. Income tax requires a Social Insurance Number and a signed return. Sales tax requires a purchase through commerce. Property tax requires ownership under Crown title. Vehicle taxes require registration and licensing. At each step, the living man or woman consents to terms. The state never proves jurisdiction. It never compels with law. It offers contracts and waits for acceptance.

The moral arguments collapse as well. Politicians claim taxes are the price of civilisation, but voluntary contributions and community service achieve more good than taxes ever have. Families support one another, neighbours share resources, and communities build without state intervention. Taxes, by contrast, fund bureaucracy, wars, and debt. The claim that taxes are noble is propaganda. The reality is that they are a commercial scheme enriching the Crown corporation and its creditors.

The Canadian tax system also exposes the global nature of control. Revenue is used to pay interest on international loans. Banks and institutions outside Canada profit more from Canadian taxes than Canadians themselves. The country is treated as a corporation within a larger corporate web. Its employees—citizens—are milked for revenue to support global creditors. This is why taxation is enforced so harshly. Without it, the Crown could not pay its masters.

Resistance does not require aggression. The sovereign approach is peaceful. By placing notices on record, by refusing joinder, by using conditional acceptance, a man or woman exposes the lack of contract. No shouting, no rebellion, no violence—only honour. This confuses the corporate system, which expects resistance to be hostile. Honour leaves it powerless. The agency cannot punish honour. It can only retreat when it cannot meet conditions.

The maxims of law again support this approach. Consent makes the law. He who fails to deny agrees. No one is obliged to accept a benefit. These truths cut through the illusions of taxation. The CRA depends on silence, on citizens accepting without question. Once you question, once you deny, once you refuse the benefit, the burden shifts to them. They cannot prove consent. They cannot produce contracts. The system unravels.

Think of how different Canada would be if more people understood this. Instead of millions signing away sovereignty each year, only a few would consent. The corporation would shrink overnight. Revenue would dry up. The Crown would lose its grip. This is why the illusion is protected so fiercely. Education, media, and threats of punishment all work together to keep Canadians compliant. But knowledge spreads, and once seen, the trick cannot be unseen.

Living as a free man or woman in Canada requires courage. The CRA will threaten, neighbours will question, and family may worry. Yet truth remains truth. Taxation is not law. It is commerce. It is consent. Once you withdraw that consent, you stand free. The corporation may rage, but it cannot compel. It can only invite, presume, and intimidate. Against knowledge and honour, it has no power.

The path forward is clear. Recognise that taxation is voluntary. Refuse to act as the Strawman. Place notices on record. Respond with conditional acceptance. Stand in honour. In doing so, you reclaim not only your wealth but your sovereignty. You remind the Crown corporation that you are not its property. You are life, born free, owing nothing to those who claim ownership through deception.

# Chapter 5: The Licence System

Every Canadian grows up believing that licences are part of life. To drive, you must obtain a driver's licence. To marry, you must secure a marriage licence. To run a business, you must register and pay for a business licence. To fish, hunt, or build, you must apply for yet more licences. From cradle to grave, permission slips define existence. People are taught to believe this is natural, that without licences society would collapse into chaos. Yet the truth is far different. Licences are not safeguards. They are contracts of servitude. They are tools used by the Crown corporation to convert natural freedoms into regulated privileges.

The very definition of a licence exposes the fraud. In legal dictionaries, a licence is permission granted by an authority to do something that would otherwise be unlawful. This definition admits that the licensed activity is lawful by nature, but the corporation declares it unlawful unless permission is purchased. In other words, the state criminalises natural actions and then sells exemptions. Canadians are tricked into believing they need permission to live their lives, when in reality they are paying fees to exercise rights they already possess by birth.

Consider driving. The ability to travel is a natural extension of freedom. A man or woman may walk, ride, or use any means to move from one place to another. Yet in Canada, travel by automobile is treated as a privilege requiring a licence. The Department of Transport declares that no one may drive without government approval. Police enforce this with tickets, fines, and even arrest. But look closer. The driver's licence is not law. It is a contract. When you apply, you agree to be bound by traffic statutes. By presenting the licence, you give police jurisdiction. Without that licence, there is no contract, and the natural right to travel remains untouched.

Examples of this truth have surfaced in Canadian courts. Individuals who challenged tickets by refusing to acknowledge driver status have forced prosecutors into confusion. Judges ask, "Are you the driver named on the licence?" When the man or woman calmly responds, "I am a traveller, not a driver engaged in commerce," the case begins to falter. This is because traffic codes apply only to those who admit to being drivers—operators of vehicles for commercial purposes. The licence is the hook. Without it, the statute has no teeth.

Marriage provides another clear example. A union between a man and woman is a private, natural act. Yet the Crown insists couples must obtain a marriage licence. By doing so, they invite the state into their relationship. Children born of the marriage are automatically registered, and the state claims interest in custody, support, and inheritance. Divorce proceedings are managed by courts because the licence created jurisdiction. Couples believe they are celebrating a sacred bond, but in truth they have entered a three-party contract: husband, wife, and the Crown. The licence ensures the Crown always has a seat at the table.

Business is also ensnared. Canadians are told they must register a business and pay for licences before trading. Yet trade is a natural right. Men and women have exchanged goods and services for millennia without permission slips. By registering a business, the individual becomes a corporate entity, subject to taxation, regulation, and inspection. They have moved from natural commerce into corporate commerce. The licence is the doorway. It transforms free trade into regulated business. The Crown then claims revenue through taxes and fees.

Hunting and fishing licences demonstrate the audacity of the scheme. For thousands of years, men and women have hunted game and caught fish to feed their families. In Canada, these acts are now criminalised unless a licence is purchased. Governments claim this protects wildlife, yet corporations are given free rein to strip forests, poison rivers, and devastate stocks. The licence does not protect nature. It protects revenue. Ordinary families are fined for catching a fish without a slip of paper, while industrial operations destroy habitats with state approval. The hypocrisy is glaring.

The licence system reaches into nearly every aspect of life. Building permits, gun licences, liquor licences, professional certifications—all are designed to create contracts with the Crown. Each one converts freedom into privilege. Each one generates revenue. Canadians are not asked if they consent to this system. They are trained to assume it is mandatory. In reality, the state cannot compel a man or woman to seek permission to live. It can only create policies and invite compliance. The trick is to disguise the invitation as law.

The language of licences always reveals their contractual nature. Forms require signatures. Fees must be paid. Conditions are attached. These are elements of contract, not of law. No statute compels you to apply for a licence. The compulsion arises only after you sign. Once you hold the licence, you are bound by its terms. Police and inspectors then enforce those terms. If you never consented, they would have no jurisdiction. The entire system relies on voluntary application.

Stories circulate of Canadians who have stood outside the licence system. Some travellers have refused to present driver's licences, demanding instead proof that travel is unlawful without them. Police often react with threats, but cases frequently collapse when pursued in honour. Farmers who sell produce directly to neighbours without business licences have succeeded by declaring their trade private. Couples who marry without state licences have recognised their unions through community and faith, leaving the Crown without jurisdiction. These examples prove that the licence system is not absolute. It depends entirely on consent.

The deeper question is why Canadians continue to submit. The answer lies in conditioning. From childhood, people are taught to equate licences with safety and legitimacy. Driver's licences are presented as proof of skill. Marriage licences are portrayed as romance. Business licences are described as professionalism. Hunting licences are sold as conservation. In reality, none of these claims hold weight. Skill is shown through practice, not permission slips. Romance is proven through devotion, not paperwork. Conservation is achieved through stewardship, not fees. The licence system is a marketing campaign designed to sell control.

The hypocrisy is further revealed by exemptions. Politicians and officials often bypass licences when it suits them. Corporations receive special permits to operate without restrictions. Government projects ignore zoning and building regulations. The licence system is enforced only against ordinary men and women. This shows that it is not about safety or order. It is about control and revenue. If licences were truly about protection, they would apply equally to all. Instead, they are selectively imposed to maintain the corporate structure.

The licence system also undermines responsibility. When people believe permission slips grant legitimacy, they stop thinking for themselves. A man with a driver's licence assumes he is safe simply because he passed a test. A builder with a permit assumes his project is sound because it was approved. Responsibility shifts from the individual to the state. This weakens honour and accountability. Sovereign men and women know that true responsibility comes from within, not from corporate approval. Licences dull that knowledge, replacing it with dependence.

The illusion of the licence system is strongest on the road. Police checkpoints, ticketing campaigns, and safety slogans bombard Canadians with the message that driving is a privilege. Yet travel is a natural right. The automobile is nothing more than an advanced form of horse and carriage, which men and women have used for centuries without permission. By redefining travel as driving, the Crown converts a right into a privilege. The licence becomes the contract. Once accepted, the individual is bound by traffic statutes, fees, and insurance schemes. Without the licence, those statutes lose their grip.

Insurance requirements expose the same trick. Provinces insist that all vehicles must be insured. The argument is that this protects others from harm. Yet harm is already addressed by natural law. If a man causes injury, he is responsible for remedy. Insurance does not replace honour. It only shifts money from families to corporations. By linking insurance to the driver's licence, the Crown ensures another revenue stream. Citizens believe they are acting responsibly, but in truth they are feeding a corporate system of profit.

The marriage licence may appear harmless, but it too has profound consequences. Couples who obtain a licence bring the state into their private union. Courts then claim jurisdiction over custody disputes, property division, and even spousal support. Children are registered automatically, strengthening the state's claim of authority. By contrast, couples who marry privately, without a state licence, retain sovereignty. Their union exists by natural law, not corporate approval. The difference is stark. One path leads to contracts with the Crown. The other preserves honour between man and woman alone.

Business licences suppress true enterprise. Every Canadian has the natural right to trade goods and services. Yet municipalities and provinces demand registration, inspection, and taxation. They argue this ensures quality and safety. In reality, it ensures control. A family who sells baked goods to neighbours can be fined for not holding a licence. A craftsman building furniture in his garage may be punished for trading without registration. These are not acts of harm. They are acts of life. By criminalising them, the Crown tightens its hold over economic freedom.

Professional licences take the deception further. Doctors, lawyers, and teachers are told they must obtain certification to practise. These certifications are licences by another name. They do not guarantee skill or integrity. They guarantee conformity. Professionals are bound by the policies of their licensing bodies, which act as arms of the Crown corporation. A doctor who questions official policy risks losing his licence. A teacher who refuses state curricula risks the same. Licences do not protect the public. They silence dissent and enforce obedience.

Building permits illustrate the absurdity. A man wishes to build a shed on his land. Natural law grants him the right to use his property. Yet the municipality demands a permit. He must submit plans, pay fees, and wait for approval. If he proceeds without permission, he risks fines or demolition. His natural right to shelter is transformed into a privilege sold back to him by the Crown. The permit is a contract that binds him to municipal codes. Without it, his right stands unchallenged. The only weapon the state holds is intimidation.

The licence system is enforced through fear, not law. Canadians obey because they fear tickets, fines, and penalties. Yet penalties apply only after consent. A ticket is an invoice, addressed to the Strawman. If the man or woman refuses joinder, the ticket collapses. Fines arise from contracts, not natural law. The threat is loud, but the foundation is weak. Once this is understood, the licence system loses much of its power.

Examples exist of Canadians who have lived outside the system. Some travel without licences, identifying themselves as living men or women when stopped. Others operate businesses privately, refusing to register. Some marry within communities of faith, ignoring state paperwork. These individuals are often harassed, threatened, or mocked. Yet many succeed in maintaining sovereignty. Their stories prove that licences are not unavoidable. They are choices, though presented as mandatory.

The persistence of the system depends on education and repetition. Children are taught that licences equal safety. Media campaigns reinforce the message with slogans: "No licence, no life," "Get your permit," "Drive safe, drive legal." None of these address truth. They are marketing lines designed to protect revenue. The Crown knows that if Canadians realised their natural rights, the licence system would collapse. By selling fear and pride, it keeps the people compliant.

The hypocrisy is undeniable. Governments grant massive exemptions to corporations while punishing individuals. Multinational companies exploit land and resources under special permits, paying token fees. Meanwhile, families are fined for trivial acts like fishing without a licence. The contrast proves that the system is not about protection. It is about profit and control. Power flows upward, while obedience is demanded downward. The licence system is the instrument of that flow.

The remedy is not anger but honour. Sovereign men and women do not refuse licences with hostility. They calmly assert their natural rights. They ask for proof of contract. They respond with notices and affidavits. They conditionally accept offers of licences if evidence is shown that such licences are required by law. When no evidence is provided, the offer falls. This approach confuses the corporation, which expects rebellion. Honour leaves it powerless. The licence system cannot function when individuals refuse to play the game.

The maxims of law again provide strength. Consent makes the law. No one is obliged to accept a benefit. He who fails to deny agrees. Applied to licences, these principles reveal the truth. By applying, you consent. By accepting, you accept the benefit. By failing to deny, you agree. The power is always in your hands. Withdraw consent, deny benefits, and demand proof. The corporation cannot respond because it has no lawful authority over life.

The licence system is perhaps the most visible form of corporate control in Canada. It touches every aspect of life, from travel to trade, from family to shelter. Yet its foundation is paper-thin. It relies entirely on consent. Once you refuse, once you stand as a living man or woman, it crumbles. The Crown may threaten, but threats are not law. Contracts are not destiny. Life is greater than paper.

Understanding the licence system is essential for sovereignty. Without this knowledge, Canadians will continue to seek permission slips for their own lives. With it, they can reclaim freedom. They can travel, trade, love, and build without begging for approval. They can stand as men and women, not as corporate entities. They can live as they were born: free, responsible, and sovereign.

# Chapter 6: Canadian Courts and Admiralty Shadows

Most Canadians believe that courts are places of justice. They imagine that judges uphold fairness, that trials seek truth, and that law protects the people. They see robes, gavels, and crests as symbols of authority. They assume courts operate on common law, grounded in history and tradition. Yet when you look closer, you find a very different reality. Canadian courts are not forums of justice. They are commercial venues, operating under Admiralty law, treating men and women as vessels in commerce.

The signs are everywhere, hidden in plain sight. The crest of the court often includes maritime symbols. The robes of judges resemble those of priests of commerce. The elevated bench symbolises a ship's bridge, from which the captain directs proceedings. The dock, where the accused stands, is the dock of a ship, where cargo is held. These are not coincidences. They are reminders that courts operate under maritime jurisdiction. The living man or woman is treated as cargo, not as sovereign.

To understand this, you must know the history of Admiralty law. Originally, it governed ships, sailors, and commerce on the seas. It dealt with contracts, cargo, and salvage. Over time, governments extended it onto land. They declared all men and women to be vessels, all property to be cargo, and all disputes to be commercial. In Canada, this transformation was complete by the twentieth century. Courts no longer apply natural law. They apply statutes and codes rooted in Admiralty principles.

The birth certificate is central to this process. When a child is registered, a maritime entity is created. The Strawman is recorded as cargo belonging to the Crown. From that moment, the courts treat the individual as a vessel engaged in commerce. Every summons, ticket, or lawsuit is addressed to the Strawman. When the man or woman answers, they step onto the ship. Jurisdiction is established. The court then proceeds not as a forum of justice but as a settlement of accounts.

Language in the courtroom reveals the deception. Judges ask, "Do you understand?" In legal terms, to understand is to stand under jurisdiction. They call the name in capital letters, waiting for response. They ask for pleas, which are forms of commercial negotiation. They speak of charges, bonds, and discharges—terms from commerce, not justice. Canadians hear these words without recognising their commercial meaning. Yet once understood, the illusion becomes obvious. The court is a marketplace, not a temple of law.

The role of the judge is not that of an impartial arbiter. He is an administrator of contracts. His task is to balance ledgers, not to uncover truth. This is why evidence of harm is often irrelevant. A man may be fined for failing to pay tax, even if no one was harmed. A woman may be punished for driving without a licence, even if no injury occurred. The harm is to the contract, not to life. The judge ensures the contract is enforced, because that is his role in the corporate system.

Lawyers are officers of this commercial court. They are members of the bar, which stands for British Accreditation Registry. Their allegiance is not to their clients but to the court. They speak in a language designed to obscure, not clarify. They negotiate settlements, rarely challenging jurisdiction. Their task is to manage the Strawman, not to defend the living man or woman. Clients who rely on lawyers often find themselves trapped, because lawyers will never expose the Admiralty nature of the court. To do so would break their oath to the system.

The dock itself is symbolic. When the accused stands there, they are treated as cargo held for processing. Bailiffs guard the dock as if protecting goods. The accused is asked to confirm their identity, which is the act of accepting the role of Strawman. Once this occurs, the trial proceeds as a commercial matter. If the accused refuses, confusion ensues. Some judges dismiss cases rather than risk exposure. The dock is not a place of honour. It is the holding bay of commerce.

Consider how fines are handled. When a court issues a fine, it is not punishing harm. It is raising revenue. The money goes to the Crown, not to any injured party. This reveals the commercial nature of the process. Fines are invoices for breach of corporate policy. They are not remedies for wrongdoing. Canadians who pay fines are feeding the corporation, not serving justice. Once seen, this truth is impossible to ignore.

Bail bonds provide another example. When someone is arrested, they may be released on bail by posting a bond. The language is commercial. A bond is a financial instrument, used in trade. The accused becomes a commodity, their freedom securitised as collateral. This practice has nothing to do with justice. It is commerce in its rawest form. The court profits from the bond, while the accused is treated as an asset.

The presence of Admiralty law explains why courts so often ignore natural justice. Canadians who claim no harm was done are brushed aside. The court is not interested in harm. It is interested in contracts. Did the accused comply with licence terms. Did they file tax forms. Did they register property. These are the questions that matter, because they are questions of commerce. Natural justice—whether anyone was injured—is irrelevant. The court has no place for it.

Cases of Canadians challenging jurisdiction expose the weakness of the system. Some have refused to answer to their names, asking instead whether the court is proceeding under Admiralty law. Judges often evade the question, knowing the truth must remain hidden. Others have demanded proof of contract before proceedings could continue. In some cases, charges were dropped rather than risk exposure. These stories are rarely reported, but they circulate among those who know. They prove that the Admiralty system is fragile, sustained only by ignorance.

The oath sworn by judges confirms their allegiance. They swear not to the people, but to the Crown. Their duty is to uphold the corporate structure, not to deliver justice. This is why courts consistently rule in favour of the state, even when evidence is weak. The Crown is always the claimant, and the judge always serves the Crown. The accused is treated as property, and the outcome is predetermined. Only by refusing joinder can a man or woman escape this trap.

The mask of justice falls most clearly when you observe how courts handle paperwork. Every case is built on documents, not living testimony. Tickets, summonses, affidavits, and motions are exchanged like contracts. Clerks stamp papers, judges read them, and rulings are written. The living voices of men and women are secondary. This reliance on paper reveals the commercial foundation. A court is not a place of truth. It is a place of record-keeping, balancing ledgers, and maintaining contracts. Life itself is pushed aside for the sake of paperwork.

The symbolism of water is another clue. Admiralty law governs the seas, and Canadian courts are drenched in maritime language. Terms like "dock," "bench," "bar," "bail," and "bond" all trace to the world of ships and trade. Even the word "court" derives from commercial gathering places, not temples of justice. When you enter a courtroom, you step onto the ship of commerce. The judge is captain, the lawyers are officers, and you are treated as cargo. Unless you refuse the role, you are processed as property.

The requirement to stand when the judge enters is part of this ritual. It is not about respect. It is about acknowledging authority. To stand is to rise as a vessel under command. To remain seated is to withhold consent, which unsettles the process. Canadians who have tested this have been threatened, but the threats reveal the fragility of the ritual. Without consent, the ceremony has no power. Courts rely on habit and fear to maintain control.

Language traps are used constantly. When a judge asks, "Do you understand," the uninformed answer yes, thinking it means comprehension. In law, it means "stand under jurisdiction." By saying yes, you accept the court's authority. Another trap is the request for a plea. To plead is to bargain. By offering a plea of guilty or not guilty, you confirm the jurisdiction of the court. The sovereign man or woman avoids these traps by calmly asking questions. "Who is being addressed. Under what jurisdiction does this court sit. Where is the contract that binds me." Such questions expose the assumption of authority.

The handling of names is another key. Cases are always opened in capital letters: R v. SMITH, or HER MAJESTY THE QUEEN v. JONES. The capitalised name refers to the Strawman. When you answer to it, you step into that role. The court then has jurisdiction. If you refuse to identify as the capitalised name, confusion arises. Judges may threaten contempt, but often they dismiss cases quietly. They do not want the public to see the truth—that jurisdiction depends entirely on voluntary joinder.

The bar itself is symbolic. It separates the gallery from the area where proceedings occur. Only lawyers, officers of the bar, may cross freely. The living man or woman must request permission. This demonstrates that the court is a private venue, controlled by a closed guild. It is not a public forum. It is a corporate chamber, accessible only to those sworn to its rules. The public are spectators, not participants. The living man or woman who crosses the bar without consent is seen as trespassing on corporate territory.

The role of police in court reinforces this structure. Sheriffs and bailiffs act as enforcers, ensuring compliance with court rules. They are not there to protect the living. They are there to protect the corporation. If an individual challenges jurisdiction, bailiffs are used to intimidate or remove them. Yet even this reveals weakness. If courts had true authority, they would not need force. The reliance on physical intimidation shows that power rests on consent, not law. Without consent, they must resort to threats, which exposes their lack of legitimacy.

The financial side of courts cannot be ignored. Every case generates revenue. Filing fees, fines, and court costs flow into government coffers. Cases are coded for accounting purposes, creating bonds that can be traded. This commercial activity is hidden from the public but well known to insiders. Courts are revenue centres, not houses of justice. They exist to sustain the Crown corporation, not to serve the people. Canadians who see this recognise that the courtroom is a marketplace disguised as law.

The treatment of debt cases illustrates the commercial nature perfectly. A bank sues a borrower, and the court enforces the contract. The borrower argues hardship or fairness, but the judge dismisses these pleas. The only issue is the contract. Did the borrower sign. Did the borrower default. If so, judgment is granted. The living man or woman is irrelevant. The contract is all that matters. This reveals that courts are not about truth or justice. They are about enforcing agreements within the corporate system, no matter the human cost.

Criminal cases follow the same pattern. A man is charged with possession of a plant. No harm has been done, no victim exists, yet the court proceeds. Why. Because statutes have defined the act as unlawful under corporate policy. The man is treated as a corporate entity bound by those policies. The court enforces the statute, not natural law. The absence of harm is ignored. The presence of a statute is enough. This shows how Admiralty shadows have overtaken common sense.

Those who have stood in honour have found ways to navigate these waters. By refusing to answer to the Strawman, by demanding proof of jurisdiction, by remaining calm and respectful, they have sometimes caused proceedings to collapse. Judges do not want the system exposed. When a man or woman insists on natural law, the court may quietly withdraw rather than risk attention. These victories are not publicised, but they are real. They prove that knowledge and honour can defeat presumption.

The greatest deception is the belief that courts protect rights. In truth, they manage contracts. The Charter is interpreted within these courts, but only to balance corporate interests. The rights of the living man or woman are never recognised, because they do not exist within the corporate framework. To seek protection from the courts is to enter the ship of commerce willingly. The sovereign man or woman avoids this trap by standing outside, refusing to board, and living in honour.

Understanding the Admiralty nature of Canadian courts is essential for sovereignty. Without this knowledge, men and women will continue to submit, believing they are receiving justice. With it, they see that they are being processed as cargo. They learn to withdraw consent, to refuse joinder, to stand as living beings. They see that the courtroom is not a place of law, but of commerce. Once the illusion is broken, the power of the court fades.

The path forward is clear. Never assume jurisdiction. Never answer blindly. Always ask for proof of contract. Always declare your standing as a living man or woman. Treat the court as what it is: a corporate ship, seeking to board you as cargo. Refuse the role. Stand in honour. When enough Canadians do this, the Admiralty shadows will dissolve, and true law—the law of the living—will rise again.

# Chapter 7: Police and RCMP - Policy Enforcers

Most Canadians believe police exist to serve and protect. They imagine officers as guardians of safety, keeping communities free from crime and danger. Schools promote this image, media reinforce it, and government slogans repeat it. Yet when you watch how police actually operate, the truth emerges. Police in Canada are not peace officers serving the people. They are policy enforcers working for the Crown corporation. Their loyalty is not to living men and women. It is to statutes, codes, and corporate interests.

The very word "police" reveals the deception. It comes from "policy." Police enforce policies written by legislatures, not laws rooted in natural justice. Natural law requires only that no one cause harm, commit fraud, or break honourable agreements. Police rarely deal with these matters. Instead, they focus on tickets, fines, regulations, and paperwork. They issue citations for parking, speeding, fishing without a licence, or failing to wear a seatbelt. These are not crimes under natural law. They are breaches of policy. The police exist to ensure compliance with those policies, because the corporation depends on obedience for revenue.

The Royal Canadian Mounted Police, presented as a symbol of national pride, are perhaps the clearest example. Their origin was to secure Crown authority over western lands, not to protect settlers or Indigenous peoples. They enforced government policy, often violently, to expand Crown control. That role has never changed. Today, RCMP officers enforce statutes across the country, from traffic codes to tax collection. They swear oaths to the Crown, not to the people. Their duty is to the corporation. Canadians who see them as community protectors misunderstand their true function.

The way police handle identification shows their role as policy enforcers. When they stop a traveller, the first demand is always for a name and identification. This is not about safety. It is about establishing joinder with the Strawman. Once the traveller presents a licence or card, the officer treats them as a corporate entity bound by statutes. Without identification, the officer struggles to proceed. This reveals that their authority does not extend to the living man or woman. It extends only to corporate entities. Identification is the hook.

Tickets provide further proof. When an officer issues a ticket, it is not a charge for harm done. It is an invoice for breach of corporate policy. The fine is payable to the Crown, not to any injured party. The language of the ticket is commercial. It lists an amount due, a due date, and a process for appeal. This is contract, not law. Canadians pay tickets because they fear escalation, not because they caused harm. Police serve as collection agents, ensuring steady revenue for the corporation.

The presence of quotas exposes this function clearly. Though often denied, many officers admit that departments expect a certain number of tickets to be issued each month. This has nothing to do with safety. It is revenue generation. Officers are pressured to stop travellers, issue citations, and fill the coffers of municipalities. The result is that police focus on minor policy breaches while serious crimes of harm and fraud often go unaddressed. This inversion of priorities proves that police are policy enforcers, not peace officers.

Peace officers once existed in Canada. Their role was to maintain peace, to intervene only when harm or breach of honour occurred. They were respected by communities because they served life, not policy. But over time, peace officers were replaced by police officers. The shift in title reflected the shift in duty. Today, the distinction remains in law: statutes still refer to peace officers. Yet in practice, nearly all have become police, enforcing codes and ignoring natural justice. The living man or woman seeking peace officers rarely finds them. They find policy enforcers in uniform.

The equipment of police reveals their purpose. Officers carry ticket books, radios, and laptops to record data and issue fines. Their cars are fitted with scanners and cameras to track compliance with registration and insurance. These are tools of revenue collection. They are not the tools of peace-making. Weapons are carried, not to protect the people, but to intimidate compliance. Uniforms are designed to project authority, ensuring citizens submit without question. Everything about the police is crafted to enforce corporate policy, not to serve human life.

The RCMP's involvement in taxation cases confirms their role. They assist the Canada Revenue Agency in enforcing tax collection, sometimes raiding businesses or seizing assets. Taxation is a commercial matter, yet armed officers enforce it. This shows that police power is not about law but about contracts. The CRA issues invoices, and police back them with force. If taxes were truly law, force would be unnecessary. Consent would suffice. The presence of police reveals the weakness of the system. It needs intimidation to maintain compliance.

Protests expose the true nature of police loyalty. When Canadians gather to voice dissent, police are deployed not to protect them but to control them. They enforce permit requirements, restrict assembly, and disperse crowds. Their goal is not to defend freedom but to maintain order for the Crown. During recent demonstrations, police arrested peaceful men and women simply for refusing to follow policy. They acted as enforcers for government agendas, silencing opposition. This is not the role of guardians of liberty. It is the role of corporate security.

The funding of police confirms their corporate identity. Budgets are provided by municipalities, provinces, and the federal government—all Crown corporations. Officers are employees, paid to enforce policies. Their pensions, benefits, and promotions depend on loyalty to the system. No officer who questions the legitimacy of statutes survives in the force. They are trained to obey orders, not to think critically. The result is an army of enforcers who serve the corporation faithfully, while believing they serve the people.

The way police speak to the public shows their assumption of authority. They issue commands: "Show me your ID," "Step out of the vehicle," "Sign here." These are offers of contract disguised as orders. If you comply, you accept. If you remain calm and ask questions, the illusion fades. "Who is being addressed. What law requires this. Am I obliged to comply." Such questions unsettle officers, because they reveal that their authority is not absolute. It is based on consent. Without that consent, they are powerless.

The tactics police use prove their role as enforcers of policy rather than guardians of peace. Roadblocks are set up not to stop violent criminals but to check licences, registrations, and insurance. Officers stand with ticket books in hand, ready to collect revenue. These checkpoints are sold to the public as safety measures, yet statistics show that they generate far more fines than they prevent accidents. The real purpose is revenue collection. A true peace officer would intervene only when harm is present. A policy enforcer intervenes constantly to ensure compliance with codes.

The arrest process reveals the same deception. When a man is arrested, he is told his rights under the Charter. These rights are not absolute. They are privileges, subject to limits. The arrest itself is based on statutes, not on natural law. A man may be taken into custody for failing to pay a fine or for disobeying an order, even though he harmed no one. This is corporate enforcement, not justice. Police act as sheriffs of the Crown, transporting cargo—the Strawman—into custody, where courts process him as property.

The RCMP's history with Indigenous peoples exposes their true function. They enforced Crown policy by removing children from families, seizing lands, and crushing resistance. These acts were not about protecting anyone. They were about expanding corporate control. The same patterns continue today when police enforce pipeline projects, seizing land from those who refuse consent. They stand with corporations against communities, proving their loyalty to policy over people. For Indigenous and non-Indigenous alike, the RCMP is a reminder that police serve the Crown first.

Language used by police officers betrays their role. They speak of "enforcing the law," but in practice they enforce statutes. They claim authority by saying "It's the law," when in reality they mean "It's policy." The difference is crucial. Natural law requires no enforcement. It is universal, self-evident, and undeniable. Statutes require armies of enforcers, because they are contracts disguised as law. Without police, statutes would be meaningless. This dependence proves they are not true law.

The use of force reveals the insecurity of the system. Officers are armed, armoured, and trained in intimidation. Peace requires none of this. Peace is maintained by respect and honour. Policy requires force. Canadians are told that weapons are for protection, but the reality is clear. The weapons are for compliance. The living man or woman who challenges jurisdiction will often face the threat of violence, not reasoned argument. The corporation knows it cannot win with truth, so it relies on intimidation.

Quotas, though denied officially, are openly acknowledged by many former officers. Departments measure productivity by tickets issued and arrests made. This is not justice. It is corporate accounting. Officers are pressured to treat citizens as revenue sources. The more fines they issue, the more they are rewarded. This explains why so many officers focus on minor infractions while major crimes remain unsolved. They are not measured by justice served. They are measured by revenue collected.

Consider how police interact with banks. When a bank forecloses on a home, police enforce the eviction. The family may have lived there for decades, yet officers arrive to remove them. No harm was caused, no crime committed, yet police stand with the bank. They are not defending peace. They are defending corporate contracts. Their loyalty is proven by action. They serve the Crown corporation and its financial allies, not the people.

Community policing is marketed as a way to build trust, yet its function is surveillance. Officers walk neighbourhoods, attend schools, and engage with families. They present themselves as friendly faces, but their role is to gather information and maintain compliance. Communities are lulled into acceptance, forgetting that these officers ultimately serve the corporation. When conflict arises, the friendly face disappears, replaced by the enforcer in uniform. The mask of service slips, revealing the true role beneath.

Media portrayal of police supports the illusion. Television dramas depict officers as heroes fighting crime. News stories highlight their bravery while downplaying their abuses. Rarely are Canadians shown the reality of ticket quotas, revenue collection, and corporate loyalty. The myth of the noble protector is carefully maintained. Those who question it are ridiculed or silenced. The illusion thrives on repetition, not truth.

Yet cracks appear. Videos of police misconduct circulate online, showing brutality against peaceful men and women. These moments reveal the truth: police are not neutral. They serve the system. When citizens stand in honour, calmly refusing consent, officers often respond with force. This proves their role as enforcers, not protectors. Honour frightens the system because it exposes its weakness. Violence is used to cover that fear.

For the sovereign man or woman, dealing with police requires knowledge and calm. The key is to avoid joinder. Do not answer as the Strawman. Do not present identification unless truly necessary. Ask questions: "Who is being addressed. Under what authority. Where is the contract." Speak respectfully but firmly. Honour disarms intimidation. Officers expect fear and submission. They do not know how to respond to knowledge calmly expressed. Some may retreat, others may escalate, but the truth remains: without consent, they have no lawful authority.

The maxims of law again provide guidance. Consent makes the law. No one is obliged to accept a benefit. Silence implies agreement. Police rely on these principles but twist them for corporate ends. They assume consent when you comply silently. They presume you accepted benefits such as licences and registrations. They claim authority because you failed to deny it. The sovereign man or woman reverses this by refusing consent, rejecting benefits, and denying assumptions. Police then face the truth: they are powerless without agreement.

Examples exist of Canadians standing firm. Travellers who calmly declared they were not drivers but men and women exercising their right to travel have seen tickets dismissed. Citizens who refused to provide identification without proof of obligation have been released without charge. Protesters who placed notices on record affirming their sovereignty have forced police to withdraw. These victories are not widely known, but they are real. They show that honour and knowledge can overcome intimidation.

The role of police in Canada is not to protect the people. It is to protect the Crown corporation. Every uniform, every badge, every oath confirms this. The RCMP's red serge is not a symbol of freedom. It is a symbol of service to the Crown. Municipal and provincial officers may wear different uniforms, but their function is the same. They enforce statutes, not natural law. They serve revenue, not justice.

Recognising this truth is essential for sovereignty. Without it, Canadians will continue to trust officers who do not serve them. With it, they can stand in honour, refusing to be intimidated. They can see officers not as guardians but as enforcers. They can adjust their conduct accordingly, always calm, always questioning, never consenting. This knowledge transforms encounters. Fear is replaced by clarity. Intimidation is met with honour.

Police and RCMP are not the enemy, but they are not friends either. They are employees of a corporation, following orders, serving masters above them. Many officers may believe they are helping, but belief does not change reality. Their loyalty is sworn to the Crown, not to the people. The sovereign man or woman remembers this always. By doing so, they navigate encounters with wisdom. They refuse contracts. They uphold natural law. They stand free.

# Chapter 8: Debt, Banks, and Mortgages

Debt is the silent chain that binds most Canadians. From the moment a young man or woman opens a bank account, takes a student loan, or signs for a credit card, the trap begins. Debt is sold as opportunity—an education, a home, a future. In truth, it is a system of servitude. Banks create money from nothing, lend it at interest, and then enforce repayment through courts and police. Canadians spend their lives working to repay figures typed into screens. The result is that generations labour not for themselves, but for banks and creditors.

The first deception lies in the creation of money. Canadians are told banks lend money from deposits, that one person's savings are used for another's loan. In reality, banks create money the moment a signature is given. The loan agreement becomes an asset on the bank's books. The amount is credited into an account, and from there it circulates as if it were real. Nothing of substance changes hands. The borrower's promise to repay is the only source of value. In other words, it is the man or woman who creates the money, not the bank.

Yet the bank charges interest on this creation. It demands repayment of more than was ever created. This ensures that debt can never be fully cleared. For every loan issued, there is more debt than money in circulation. The result is a constant scramble, with individuals, families, and businesses fighting to earn enough to pay interest. Those who fall behind face foreclosure, repossession, and bankruptcy. This cycle is not accidental. It is the design of the system. Debt is the product, and enslavement is the outcome.

Mortgages are the sharpest tool in this system. Canadians are told that buying a home is the path to security. They are told to sign a mortgage, which literally means "death pledge." The word reveals the truth. A mortgage is a pledge that endures until death or until the bank is satisfied. When a man or woman signs, they believe they are borrowing money. In fact, they are creating credit with their signature. The bank takes that signature, treats it as an asset, and then demands repayment with interest. The borrower spends decades paying back what they themselves created.

Ownership under a mortgage is an illusion. The title of the property remains with the bank until the pledge is fulfilled. Even then, the land is not truly owned. It remains under Crown title, with property tax owed annually. Failure to pay allows the municipality to seize the land. The Canadian who believes he owns his home is in truth a tenant twice over—first to the bank, then to the Crown. This double layer of servitude ensures that true independence through land ownership is impossible under the corporate system.

Credit cards extend the same deception. They offer immediate access to goods in exchange for future repayment. Yet the repayment demanded always exceeds what was borrowed, due to interest. Those who cannot keep up are trapped in cycles of minimum payments, where the debt never shrinks. Banks profit endlessly, feeding on families who never escape the cycle. The living man or woman is reduced to a debtor, working to sustain a corporate system that gave nothing of value in return.

Student loans target the young. Promised that education is the key to success, students sign agreements before they understand the system. They emerge with tens of thousands in debt, owing money that never truly existed. Interest piles on, and their working lives begin not with freedom but with chains. For many, repayment lasts decades. The result is that the most promising years of life are spent serving banks, rather than building independence. The very system that claims to empower youth begins by enslaving them.

The enforcement of debt exposes its commercial nature. When a borrower falls behind, banks turn to courts. The case is not about harm. No one was injured. The bank lent nothing of substance. Yet the court enforces the contract. The judge treats the borrower as the Strawman, bound by agreement. The living man or woman is ignored. The contract rules. Police may then enforce eviction or seizure, ensuring compliance. The cycle is clear: the bank creates credit from your signature, the court enforces the contract, and the police ensure compliance. It is a corporate triangle of control.

Consider how banks profit from defaults. When a mortgage holder fails to pay, the bank seizes the property. It then sells the home, often for more than the balance owed. The borrower loses both the property and years of payments, while the bank profits again. The same occurs with vehicles and other assets. Repossession is not punishment. It is profit. The system is designed to ensure banks win, whether payments are made or not. The borrower always loses, because they never truly owned what they believed was theirs.

The illusion of credit ratings adds another layer. Credit bureaus track every payment, late fee, and balance. They assign scores that determine whether banks will issue more debt. Canadians live in fear of damaging their scores, because without credit they cannot rent homes, buy cars, or secure jobs. This is another form of control. The score is not a measure of character. It is a measure of obedience to debt. Those who comply are rewarded with more chains. Those who resist are punished with exclusion. The system enforces servitude by rewarding the most compliant debtors.

Debt is often justified as necessary for progress. Politicians claim that without borrowing, Canadians could not buy homes, start businesses, or study. Yet history shows otherwise. Communities thrived long before banks monopolised credit. Families built homes together. Farmers exchanged goods and services. Education was shared through apprenticeship and community schools. The corporate system replaced cooperation with debt, ensuring profit for banks at the expense of freedom. What once was free is now sold with interest.

The morality of debt is weak. Charging interest on money created from nothing is usury, condemned throughout history. Ancient scriptures, common law traditions, and moral teachings all warned against it. Yet in Canada, it is legal, encouraged, and celebrated. Banks are praised as pillars of society, even as they drain wealth from families. The truth is that debt is theft disguised as contract. It extracts labour and wealth without giving anything of substance in return.

For the sovereign man or woman, the remedy begins with knowledge. Recognise that loans are not gifts from banks. They are creations of your own signature. Recognise that mortgages do not grant ownership. They are pledges of servitude. Recognise that courts and police serve the banks, not justice. Once this is clear, the illusion begins to fade. You may still face pressure, but you see it for what it is: commerce, not law.

The enforcement of debt is perhaps the clearest example of how Canadian courts and police act as extensions of the banking system. When a borrower defaults, banks rarely negotiate in honour. Instead, they file claims in court. The language of the claim is commercial. It cites agreements, balances, and defaults, never harm or injury. Judges almost always side with the bank, because their role is to enforce contracts. The borrower is treated as the Strawman, bound by signature. The living man or woman is invisible in this process.

Police then step in to enforce judgments. Families are removed from homes, vehicles are seized, wages are garnished. Officers act as muscle for banks, ensuring compliance with contracts that were fraudulent from the start. The irony is striking: the bank lent nothing of substance, yet the borrower loses everything. Courts and police ensure that fraud is dressed as law. The borrower's labour and life are sacrificed to protect the illusion that banks have power.

The cycle is reinforced by propaganda. Canadians are told debt is a tool, that mortgages build wealth, and that credit cards offer convenience. Advertising portrays debt as freedom, not slavery. A couple smiles as they sign a mortgage. Students celebrate receiving loans. Families rejoice at buying cars with credit. The reality is hidden: decades of repayment, endless interest, and the constant threat of repossession. The smiling faces are masks for chains.

Even government participates in this deception. Politicians encourage home ownership through incentives, knowing it traps citizens in mortgages. They promote student loans to expand access to education, knowing it shackles youth with debt. They support banks as "too big to fail," ensuring that citizens bear the cost of bailouts. The Crown corporation and the banking cartel work hand in hand, feeding off the labour of Canadians. The people believe they are free, but their wages are pledged to banks from the moment they sign.

The scale of this debt trap is staggering. Canadian households hold some of the highest levels of debt in the world. Mortgages, credit cards, auto loans, and student loans consume the majority of income. Families work not for themselves but for creditors. The system is designed this way. Debt keeps citizens obedient. Those who owe cannot easily resist. They fear losing homes, jobs, and reputations. Debt is the perfect tool of control, stronger than chains or bars.

The creation of money from signatures is the system's most guarded secret. Banks know that if Canadians realised they create credit themselves, the illusion would collapse. Every promissory note, loan agreement, or mortgage contract is monetised by the bank. The borrower provides the value, and the bank profits. The borrower is never told this. Instead, they are led to believe the bank provided something of worth. In truth, the bank risked nothing. The living man or woman is the true source of wealth. The bank merely exploits their ignorance.

Foreclosure cases highlight the cruelty. A family falls behind by a few payments. The bank moves swiftly, filing claims, obtaining judgments, and seizing the property. Years of payments are lost, equity is erased, and the family is left homeless. The bank then sells the property, often at a profit. No sympathy, no honour, only commerce. The family is treated as collateral, their lives reduced to figures on a balance sheet. The courts bless the process, and police enforce it. This is not justice. It is corporate plunder.

Credit ratings are used to reinforce obedience. A low score prevents access to housing, employment, and further loans. Canadians fear damaging their scores, so they comply with unreasonable demands. They pay late fees, interest, and penalties to protect numbers on a screen. The score does not measure honour or integrity. It measures compliance. Those who obey banks are rewarded. Those who resist are punished. It is a system of behavioural control disguised as financial responsibility.

The sovereign man or woman sees debt for what it is: illusion. They recognise that banks lend nothing of substance. They know that their signature created the credit. They see that courts and police enforce contracts, not law. With this knowledge, they approach debt differently. They may use notices, affidavits, and conditional acceptance to challenge claims. They may remind banks that no lawful consideration was given. They may demand proof that a loan was backed by real assets. When proof cannot be provided, the claim collapses. Honour is preserved, and the fraud is exposed.

This does not mean the path is easy. Banks will resist. Courts will mock. Police will threaten. Families and friends may not understand. Yet the truth remains. Debt is fraud disguised as contract. By standing firm, by refusing to consent blindly, by demanding evidence, the sovereign man or woman can resist. Even small victories matter, because they expose weakness in the system. Each unanswered notice, each dismissed claim, is proof that the fraud cannot withstand honour.

The moral case against debt is strong. For centuries, usury was condemned. To charge interest on money was seen as theft. Only in modern times has it been normalised. Banks and governments claim it is necessary for progress, but history proves otherwise. Communities once built without debt, families once thrived without mortgages, and youth once learned without loans. The introduction of debt was not for progress. It was for profit. Canadians have been deceived into believing slavery is freedom.

The way forward is to reclaim responsibility. Instead of depending on banks, families can trade directly, build together, and share knowledge. Communities can support one another without debt. Individuals can refuse unnecessary credit, relying on honour instead of contracts. Sovereign men and women can remind banks that life is greater than paper. Debt may dominate today, but it survives only because people believe in it. Withdraw belief, and it collapses.

Debt, banks, and mortgages are the foundation of the Crown corporation's control. They ensure Canadians remain obedient, working lifetimes for creditors. They transform signatures into chains, promises into pledges, and homes into collateral. Yet once exposed, the fraud loses power. A man or woman who knows the truth cannot be enslaved. They may face hardship, but they remain free in spirit. Freedom begins with knowledge, and knowledge reveals that debt is an illusion.

# Chapter 9: Education and Programming in Canada

Every society depends on teaching its young. In free communities, elders once taught children honour, responsibility, and practical skills. Knowledge was passed through families, trades, and traditions. Children learned to respect natural law, to live by truth, and to care for one another. In Canada today, that ancient model has been replaced by a corporate system of programming. Schools no longer serve life. They serve the Crown corporation, shaping children into obedient citizens who accept debt, taxation, and licences without question.

The design of modern education reveals its purpose. From the first day of kindergarten, children are placed in rows, taught to sit still, and trained to obey authority. They raise their hands to speak, ask permission to move, and memorise lessons repeated by teachers. This is not natural learning. It is conditioning. The child learns that knowledge comes from above, that rules cannot be questioned, and that compliance is rewarded. These lessons last long after school ends. The adult who once sat quietly in class grows into a citizen who obeys government orders without resistance.

Curricula are crafted not to empower but to control. Canadian schools focus heavily on citizenship, rights under the Charter, and duties to government. Children learn to salute the flag, to recite national history, and to celebrate the Charter as the source of freedom. Rarely are they told that true freedom comes by birth, not by statute. Instead, they are taught to see themselves as citizens—a role that exists only within the Crown corporation. By the time they reach adulthood, most Canadians cannot imagine life outside this framework. They are programmed to equate citizenship with identity.

Mathematics and literacy are taught, but always with a view toward future employment. Schools emphasise skills useful to corporations, not wisdom useful to life. Practical skills like gardening, carpentry, and household management are ignored. Instead, children are trained for exams, grades, and credentials. Success is defined as entry into higher education, which leads to student loans and debt. From classroom to lecture hall, the path is paved with contracts. The child grows into a worker, not a free man or woman.

Discipline in schools also reflects corporate priorities. Rules are strict, punishments harsh, and individuality discouraged. Children who resist are labelled disruptive or disobedient. Increasingly, they are diagnosed with behavioural disorders and medicated. This medicalisation of resistance ensures compliance. A child who questions authority is not celebrated for independence. He is silenced with pills. The system cannot tolerate sovereignty, even in youth. It demands obedience at all costs.

History lessons provide some of the strongest examples of programming. Students are taught a version of Canadian history that glorifies government and hides Crown control. They learn of Confederation, of prime ministers, of wars and treaties. They do not learn that Canada remains under Crown authority. They do not learn that the Charter is a corporate licence, not a declaration of freedom. They do not learn that natural law predates government. By shaping history, the system shapes identity. Children believe their ancestors fought for freedom, when in truth they were bound to the same corporate system that binds them today.

Civic education completes the cycle. Students are encouraged to vote, to trust courts, and to respect police. They are told these institutions are pillars of democracy. Rarely are they invited to question whether democracy exists at all. Rarely are they asked to examine whether courts serve justice or commerce. Rarely are they told that police enforce policy, not law. Instead, they are given a story that makes obedience appear noble. The programming ensures that by adulthood, most Canadians defend the very system that enslaves them.

The role of media in education cannot be ignored. Television, films, and news reinforce the same messages. Heroes are portrayed as soldiers, police, and politicians. Rebels are mocked or demonised. Advertisements celebrate consumerism, teaching children that happiness comes from spending. Music and entertainment distract from deeper questions. Together, school and media create a closed loop of programming. The child grows into an adult who consumes, obeys, and rarely questions. The sovereign voice is silenced before it ever emerges.

Teachers themselves are not to blame individually. Many enter the profession with noble intentions, believing they are serving children. Yet they are bound by curricula designed by ministries of education. Their careers depend on compliance. Those who question the system risk discipline or dismissal. They are policy enforcers in classrooms, much like police on the streets. They deliver programming faithfully, often unaware of the deeper structure. The system ensures its survival by capturing not only students but also educators.

Examinations and grading are further tools of control. Children are told their worth depends on marks, that failure is shameful, and that success comes from pleasing authority. This creates adults who fear failure and seek approval. They avoid risk, question little, and strive for security within the system. Sovereignty requires courage, but schools teach conformity. By design, few graduates have the strength to stand against corporate authority. They have been programmed to submit.

Universities intensify this conditioning. Students are taught to specialise in narrow fields, focusing on technical skills rather than broad wisdom. They are encouraged to accept debt as normal, to compete for grades, and to pursue careers in service to corporations. Those who challenge orthodoxies are marginalised. Research funding is tied to government and corporate priorities. Professors who dissent risk losing support. The result is that higher education produces servants of the system, not free thinkers.

The programming even extends to language. Children are taught to use terms like "citizen," "taxpayer," and "resident" without question. They are told these words define identity. They are not told these are corporate roles tied to the Strawman. By the time they reach adulthood, most Canadians describe themselves with corporate labels. They have forgotten they are living men and women. The language of education becomes the language of slavery.

The conditioning of Canadian education is not limited to classrooms. It extends into every stage of life, ensuring that programming continues long after formal schooling ends. Governments provide adult learning courses, workplace training, and professional certifications. These appear to offer advancement but in reality they reinforce dependence. Adults are told they must continually upgrade skills to remain employable. They are reminded that credentials, not experience, define worth. This never-ending cycle ensures that individuals remain trapped in corporate systems, always seeking approval from authorities.

One of the most damaging aspects of programming is the removal of critical thinking. Children are taught to memorise, not to question. They are rewarded for repeating answers, not for exploring possibilities. Those who think differently are marginalised, labelled as daydreamers or troublemakers. The sovereign spirit thrives on questions, but schools suffocate it. By adulthood, most Canadians have lost the ability to challenge authority. They may complain about taxes or bureaucracy, but they never question the legitimacy of the system itself. That power of inquiry has been trained out of them.

Consider the ritual of pledging allegiance to the flag or singing the national anthem. These acts appear harmless, but they are rituals of loyalty to the Crown corporation. Children repeat them daily, embedding the idea that they are subjects of the state. Rarely are they told that true allegiance belongs only to natural law and to life itself. By the time they are adults, these rituals have shaped their identity. They believe they belong to the corporation, because they were programmed to believe it from the start.

The handling of Indigenous history in Canadian schools reveals the bias of programming. Textbooks speak of reconciliation, but rarely explain the role of the Crown in seizing land, enforcing residential schools, and suppressing sovereignty. Indigenous teachings about natural law, honour, and community responsibility are ignored. Instead, students are taught a sanitised version of history that legitimises Crown authority. This programming ensures that both Indigenous and non-Indigenous students grow up believing the Crown has lawful title to the land, when in truth it seized it through deception and violence.

Discipline practices also reflect corporate goals. Detention, suspension, and expulsion are used to enforce compliance. Children who resist are not engaged with compassion but punished into submission. The message is clear: obey or suffer consequences. This prepares them for adult life under statutes, where disobedience is met with fines, tickets, and imprisonment. Schools are training grounds for the larger system, conditioning children to accept punishment as the natural result of questioning authority.

Programming extends through subtle lessons as well. The ringing of bells trains children to respond to external commands. The grading of behaviour teaches them to value obedience over curiosity. Group projects emphasise conformity, discouraging independent thought. These methods create adults who are comfortable in offices, factories, and bureaucracies—environments where obedience is rewarded and individuality suppressed. The design is deliberate. Schools are factories producing compliant citizens, not free men and women.

The content of economics and civics courses provides further evidence. Students are taught that taxes are necessary, that debt fuels growth, and that licences protect the public. Rarely are they shown the fraud behind these systems. They are told that government is a protector, not a corporation. They are told that banks provide money, not that money is created by signatures. They are told that courts deliver justice, not that they operate under Admiralty law. By presenting illusions as facts, education cements the corporate worldview.

Media entertainment plays a supporting role. Films glorify police, soldiers, and politicians. Television portrays rebels as criminals or fools. News outlets repeat government lines, shaping public opinion. Schools and media work together, creating a seamless web of programming. Children learn in class that government is good. They turn on the television and see the same message. By adulthood, the programming is complete. The citizen defends the system with pride, never realising they were conditioned from birth.

The financial structure of education also reveals its purpose. Student loans trap youth in debt before they begin adult life. Universities charge high tuition, forcing students to borrow. By the time they graduate, they are bound by repayment schedules that last decades. This debt ensures compliance. A young graduate who owes tens of thousands is unlikely to challenge the system. They are too busy working to repay loans. The debt is not accidental. It is a deliberate extension of programming into economic control.

Teachers' unions and ministries of education also serve the system. They negotiate wages and conditions but never question the purpose of education itself. They ensure teachers remain focused on delivering curricula, not challenging it. When dissent arises, it is silenced. Teachers who question programming risk discipline. Those who comply are rewarded with pensions and stability. The structure ensures loyalty to the corporation at every level.

Yet despite this, cracks appear. Some teachers quietly encourage critical thinking, urging students to ask questions. Some parents withdraw children from schools, choosing homeschooling or alternative education. Some communities revive traditions of natural learning, teaching skills, honour, and sovereignty outside the state system. These efforts are small, but they show that programming can be resisted. Sovereignty begins with education, and reclaiming it requires breaking free from corporate schooling.

For the sovereign man or woman, the lesson is clear. Do not accept education as truth without question. Recognise it as programming. Teach children natural law: cause no harm, commit no fraud, honour your agreements. Teach them practical skills: how to grow food, build shelter, and trade fairly. Teach them honour and responsibility. These lessons build free men and women, not citizens. They prepare children for sovereignty, not servitude.

The future of Canada depends on breaking the cycle of programming. If each generation is trained to be obedient citizens, the corporation will endure. If even a few are raised as sovereign men and women, the illusion weakens. Knowledge spreads, honour grows, and freedom returns. The classroom may be the strongest tool of the Crown, but it can also be the place where its power begins to crumble.

Education and programming are not the same. Education serves life. Programming serves the corporation. Canadians must learn to see the difference. Once seen, the choice is simple. Refuse programming. Embrace true education. Raise children to be sovereign, and the system loses its hold. The future belongs to those who remember that life, not paper, is the source of freedom.

# Chapter 10: Media and Perception in Canada

Media is the most powerful tool of control in modern Canada. Governments and corporations can pass statutes, impose taxes, and issue fines, but without the consent of the people, these measures fail. Consent is secured through perception, and perception is shaped by media. Television, newspapers, radio, and now digital platforms form a constant stream of messages that condition Canadians to accept the authority of the Crown corporation. Media does not simply report reality. It manufactures it.

The structure of Canadian media reveals its allegiance. The Canadian Broadcasting Corporation (CBC) is funded by the federal government, which is itself a Crown corporation. Private networks depend on licences issued by the same government, as well as advertising from major corporations tied to banks and global interests. This means every outlet is bound to serve corporate and state priorities. No media company can operate freely when its survival depends on approval from the very system it is supposed to scrutinise.

Content reflects this control. News stories consistently portray government as protector, courts as impartial, and police as guardians. Dissenters are portrayed as extremists, radicals, or conspiracy theorists. Rarely are their arguments examined fairly. When protests occur, cameras focus on conflict, painting demonstrators as unruly. When citizens question taxes, licences, or debt, their concerns are dismissed as fringe. Media shapes perception by controlling not only what is reported but how it is framed. The people are guided to trust the corporation and distrust anyone who challenges it.

Entertainment media plays an equal role. Films and television dramas glorify police, soldiers, and lawyers. Heroes are shown as defenders of law and order, while villains are rebels or independent thinkers. This constant diet of stories trains viewers to associate authority with safety and independence with danger. Even children's programming carries these messages. Characters are praised for following rules and punished for disobedience. From cartoons to crime dramas, the message is the same: obey the system and you will be safe.

Advertising reinforces obedience through consumerism. Canadians are told happiness comes from buying, borrowing, and consuming. Banks sponsor commercials showing families smiling as they receive mortgages. Credit card companies present debt as freedom. Government agencies run campaigns praising taxes as the price of civilisation. These messages shape desires and fears. Citizens work harder, spend more, and comply with regulations because they believe their happiness depends on it. Media ensures that obedience is not only accepted but celebrated.

During crises, media control intensifies. Governments use news outlets to spread fear, justify restrictions, and silence dissent. Emergencies are declared, and media dutifully repeats official lines. Those who question measures are ridiculed as irresponsible. Courts and police enforce restrictions while media shapes public opinion to support them. This pattern has repeated in every crisis, proving that media is not an independent check on power. It is an arm of the Crown corporation, ensuring compliance.

Language used by media reveals its programming function. Words like "illegal," "mandatory," and "the law" are repeated constantly, equating statutes with natural law. Terms like "taxpayer," "citizen," and "resident" are used as if they define identity. Those who reject these labels are called "sovereign citizens," a phrase crafted to sound absurd. By controlling language, media controls thought. Canadians who hear these words daily adopt them without question, reinforcing the corporate worldview.

The handling of financial news is especially revealing. Media reports on stock markets, interest rates, and government budgets as if they are natural forces. Little attention is paid to the fraud of money creation or the usury of debt. Banks are portrayed as pillars of stability, not predators. When crises occur, media blames individuals for borrowing too much, never banks for creating fraudulent credit. This ensures that responsibility is always placed on citizens, never on the corporation.

Social media adds a new layer of control. Platforms censor dissenting voices, label alternative views as misinformation, and promote official narratives. Algorithms push mainstream content while burying challenges to the system. Canadians are told social media is free and open, but in reality it is tightly controlled. The same corporations that own traditional media influence digital platforms. The result is a seamless web of perception management, from television screens to smartphones.

The sovereign man or woman sees through this illusion. They recognise that media is not neutral. It is a tool of programming, shaping beliefs to secure consent. They understand that stories of safety, duty, and citizenship are narratives, not truths. They know that ridicule of dissent is deliberate, designed to isolate and silence. With this awareness, they no longer accept media at face value. They question, research independently, and rely on honour, not headlines.

The greatest strength of media is repetition. Canadians hear the same messages daily: obey the law, trust government, pay taxes, rely on banks, respect police. Over time, repetition becomes belief. Few stop to question whether statutes are law, whether taxes are voluntary, whether banks create money from nothing, or whether police serve people rather than the Crown. Repetition drowns out doubt. It conditions citizens to accept illusions as reality.

Ridicule is another powerful weapon. When sovereign men and women speak truth, media brands them extremists or cranks. News anchors smirk, comedians mock, and newspapers print dismissive headlines. This ridicule is designed not to disprove but to discourage. Many Canadians fear being mocked more than they fear being enslaved. They stay silent rather than risk ridicule. This is why media spends so much energy attacking dissenters—it keeps others from following their example.

Crisis coverage exposes media's obedience to power most clearly. During emergencies, reporters act as mouthpieces for officials. They repeat government statements without investigation. They promote fear, urging citizens to comply with restrictions. Alternative views are censored or vilified. This pattern shows that media does not serve truth. It serves policy. When fear is needed to secure obedience, media supplies it. Canadians comply, believing they are informed, when in reality they are manipulated.

Ownership structures of media companies confirm this allegiance. Major outlets are controlled by a handful of corporations with ties to banks, resource companies, and global institutions. Their interests align with the Crown corporation, not with the people. Journalists who challenge these interests often lose their jobs. Stories critical of banks, courts, or government rarely reach the public. The result is a narrow range of acceptable opinions, all supporting the system. Canadians mistake this for free press, when it is corporate propaganda.

The entertainment industry also plays a subtle role. Films glorify soldiers who fight for Crown interests abroad, police who enforce statutes at home, and lawyers who win cases within Admiralty courts. Villains are often portrayed as rebels against authority. This conditioning shapes perception subconsciously. Viewers internalise the idea that authority equals safety and rebellion equals chaos. By consuming these stories, Canadians absorb the corporate worldview without realising it.

Children's programming is especially important. Cartoons teach children to obey rules, trust authority figures, and report misbehaviour. Characters who follow orders are praised, while those who question are punished. These lessons prepare children for life as citizens. They learn to seek approval from teachers, bosses, and officials. Sovereignty is replaced by submission. Media begins conditioning before children can even read, ensuring that by adulthood the corporate worldview feels natural.

Advertising drives consumerism, which strengthens dependence on banks. Commercials link happiness to credit cards, mortgages, and loans. Families smile in new homes, students celebrate with new debt, travellers rejoice with credit purchases. The message is constant: debt equals freedom. In truth, debt equals servitude. But when media repeats the opposite long enough, citizens believe it. They borrow willingly, enslaving themselves while smiling at screens.

Independent voices exist, but they are drowned out. Small publications, websites, and broadcasters attempt to share truth, but they are censored, ridiculed, or buried by algorithms. Funding is scarce because advertisers fear association with dissent. Social media platforms flag alternative content as misinformation, steering users back to mainstream sources. This proves that free speech exists only within corporate limits. Voices of sovereignty are tolerated only at the margins, never in the mainstream.

Yet perception can be broken. When Canadians witness contradictions firsthand, media loses credibility. When courts rule against obvious justice, when taxes rise without visible benefit, when police enforce unjust policies, cracks appear. Those who have experienced injustice stop believing media narratives. They see truth with their own eyes. Once trust is lost, propaganda fails. This is why the system fights so hard to maintain credibility. Media is its most valuable weapon. Without it, obedience would collapse.

The sovereign man or woman must therefore treat media with caution. Do not consume it passively. Analyse every story. Ask: who benefits from this message. What is being left unsaid. Why is dissent ridiculed rather than debated. By asking these questions, the illusion weakens. Honour requires discernment, and discernment begins with rejecting corporate narratives.

The maxims of law remind us that silence implies agreement. When citizens accept media stories without question, they consent to deception. When they speak out, they deny consent. This is why the sovereign voice matters. Each question, each challenge, each refusal to accept propaganda chips away at the illusion. Media loses power when people stop believing.

The truth is simple: Canadian media is not free. It is an instrument of the Crown corporation, designed to shape perception, secure consent, and suppress dissent. It glorifies authority, ridicules rebels, and sells debt as freedom. It is not a mirror of reality. It is a mask. To live as a sovereign man or woman, you must see through the mask. You must trust your own eyes, your own honour, your own experience. When you do, media loses its grip. The illusion fades, and sovereignty re-emerges.

# Chapter 11: Notices, Affidavits, and Conditional Acceptance

The greatest weapon of the sovereign man or woman is not violence or rebellion. It is paperwork. Courts, banks, and governments exist in commerce. They operate through documents, contracts, and records. Their power rests on presumption, on silence being taken as agreement. The remedy is to place truth on the record in writing. When done with honour, notices and affidavits become stronger than any statute. They shift the burden of proof onto the claimant, exposing the fraud at the heart of the system.

A notice is a declaration. It is not a plea or a request. It is a statement of truth issued by a living man or woman. When you send a notice, you place your position on the record. You state what is true for you, what you accept, and what you refuse. The recipient is given opportunity to respond. If they do not, their silence is taken as agreement. This principle is ancient in commerce: he who fails to deny agrees. By using notices, sovereign men and women turn the tables. They require the corporation to prove authority, rather than assuming it exists.

An affidavit is even stronger. It is a sworn statement of truth. In commerce, an unrebutted affidavit stands as fact. Courts and agencies cannot simply ignore it. If they do not respond with equal or greater claim, the affidavit becomes law between the parties. This is why affidavits are so powerful for the sovereign. They expose presumption, deny false claims, and create a record of truth. When you stand in honour and put your word on paper, you step into the highest position in commerce.

Conditional acceptance is another key tool. It is the art of never refusing and never agreeing blindly. When a demand arrives—whether a tax bill, a licence requirement, or a court summons—the sovereign man or woman does not argue or ignore. They accept on condition that proof of claim is provided. The Canada Revenue Agency is asked to show the contract binding a living being to pay income tax. A police officer is asked to provide evidence that travel requires a licence. A court is asked to prove jurisdiction over the living man. The condition cannot be met, because no such proof exists. The demand collapses, honour is preserved, and consent is withheld.

These methods are not theory. They have been applied by men and women across Canada with success. A traveller issued a ticket responded with conditional acceptance, asking the officer to prove that he was acting as a driver in commerce. The matter was quietly dropped. A business owner challenged tax assessments with affidavits demanding evidence of obligation. The agency never replied, and the assessments were abandoned. Such victories are rarely reported, but they reveal the weakness of the system. It survives only when men and women remain silent.

The power of paperwork lies in its permanence. Words spoken in court can be twisted or ignored. Documents filed on the record cannot be erased. They remain as evidence, binding in commerce. This is why governments and banks rely so heavily on signatures. A signed contract binds, unless rebutted. Sovereigns use the same principle in reverse. They issue notices and affidavits, placing truth on the record. Silence from the other side is agreement. In this way, the living man or woman commands the field.

Honour is essential. Notices must be written calmly, respectfully, and clearly. They are not threats or arguments. They are statements of truth. Conditional acceptance is not defiance. It is willingness to comply if lawful proof is shown. Affidavits are not complaints. They are facts sworn under penalty of perjury. Honour gives these tools strength. Without honour, they are dismissed as frivolous. With honour, they carry the weight of law in commerce.

The structure of a notice is simple. It begins by identifying who is sending it: a living man or woman. It states the facts as you know them. It sets out your position: for example, that no contract exists binding you to pay tax. It gives the recipient time to respond. It warns that silence will be taken as agreement. It is signed and dated. Once sent, it shifts the burden. The claimant must reply or concede. Few can reply without exposing fraud.

Affidavits follow a stricter form. They must be sworn or affirmed before a commissioner or notary. They must state facts clearly and truthfully. They must be signed and sealed. Once filed, they stand as fact unless rebutted by another affidavit. This is why agencies fear them. An unrebutted affidavit cannot be dismissed. It becomes the highest form of evidence in commerce. Sovereigns who master affidavits hold power greater than lawyers or judges. They speak truth on the record, and no corporate officer can answer.

Conditional acceptance requires discipline. It is tempting to refuse outright or to argue aggressively. That path leads to conflict and dishonour. Conditional acceptance avoids this. It shows willingness to comply if lawful proof exists. It exposes fraud without hostility. For example: "I accept your offer to pay income tax upon proof of contract between myself, a living man, and your agency." No such proof exists. The demand falls. Honour remains intact.

These tools work because the system itself relies on them. Governments issue notices of assessment. Banks issue affidavits of debt. Courts issue summonses. These are all commercial documents. The sovereign simply mirrors the process, using the same rules in reverse. Commerce recognises only documents, signatures, and silence. By mastering paperwork, sovereign men and women fight the system on its own ground and win.

The importance of timelines cannot be overstated. A notice or affidavit always gives the recipient time to reply—perhaps 10 or 21 days. If no reply is received, the matter is closed. The silence becomes agreement. This principle is ancient, rooted in merchant law. It is respected even in modern courts, though judges try to conceal it. Timelines ensure that truth, once stated, cannot be ignored indefinitely. It becomes binding fact.

The effectiveness of notices and affidavits depends on precision. They must be worded with care, free of emotion, and rooted in fact. Angry rants or vague claims weaken the position. The sovereign man or woman must always speak clearly and truthfully. If you claim no contract exists, you must be ready to stand by that truth. If you state you are a living man or woman, you must never contradict yourself by acting as the Strawman. Consistency is key. Once on the record, your words define the standing of the matter.

Conditional acceptance also requires patience. Agencies and corporations often reply with threats, automated letters, or unrelated forms. These are attempts to intimidate or distract. They are not proper rebuttals. The sovereign must remain calm. Reply once more, pointing out that the original conditions have not been met. If silence follows, the matter is closed. At that point, your truth stands as fact. Many give up too soon, believing silence means defeat. In commerce, silence after notice means agreement. The key is to persist with honour until the timeline ends.

Some Canadians have seen remarkable results using these tools. A man who received repeated tax demands responded each time with conditional acceptance, asking for the signed contract binding him as a taxpayer. The agency replied with threats but never produced a contract. After three rounds of notices, silence followed. The matter ended. Another Canadian challenged a bank by filing an affidavit of truth, stating that the bank lent nothing of substance and demanding proof to the contrary. No rebuttal came. The affidavit stood as fact. The debt claim collapsed.

These victories are rarely celebrated publicly, because they threaten the system. Courts, banks, and governments do not want Canadians to know how powerful paperwork can be. They rely on ignorance. Lawyers mock those who use notices and affidavits, calling them frivolous. Judges attempt to ignore them. Yet behind closed doors, silence is proof that the claim cannot be answered. The sovereign who stands in honour and uses paperwork properly often succeeds, even if the victory is quiet.

Honour also protects against accusations of evasion. When you refuse outright to pay taxes or obey statutes, the corporation portrays you as lawless. When you conditionally accept, you demonstrate good faith. You show willingness to comply if lawful proof exists. This places the burden on the other side. If they cannot meet the condition, the failure is theirs. Honour shields you, proving that you did not refuse duty—you demanded truth. This distinction is vital. It is the difference between rebellion and sovereignty.

Affidavits hold unique power because they are sworn. In commerce, nothing stands higher than an unrebutted affidavit. Courts know this, which is why they try to dismiss them as irrelevant. Yet dismissal is not rebuttal. If no counter-affidavit is filed, the facts stand. A man who swears that he is not the corporate entity named in a case and that no contract binds him cannot be lawfully contradicted unless another sworn statement is filed. Judges may ignore, but silence remains agreement. This is why affidavits frighten the system. They expose fraud with undeniable force.

It is important to remember that paperwork alone is not enough. The man or woman must also live in honour. If you swear an affidavit but then act as a taxpayer, you undermine your position. If you declare you are not a driver but then present a driver's licence, you contradict yourself. Sovereignty requires consistency. Your actions must align with your words. Notices and affidavits are powerful only when backed by a life lived in truth. Hypocrisy destroys credibility. Honour sustains it.

The process of sending notices teaches discipline. Each step requires clarity, patience, and faith in truth. Writing calmly, giving timelines, and standing firm builds character. Many who begin this path discover that the paperwork is not only a tool but also a training ground. It teaches the sovereign to think clearly, to act with honour, and to remain calm under pressure. These qualities matter as much as the documents themselves. The system thrives on fear and confusion. Sovereignty thrives on knowledge and composure.

Critics argue that these methods never work, pointing to cases where judges ignored affidavits or dismissed notices. What critics ignore is that dismissal is not rebuttal. A judge may try to sweep aside a notice, but silence in commerce still equals agreement. The fact remains on the record. Even if ignored, it stands. Sovereigns know that victory is not always immediate or visible. Sometimes it is the quiet absence of further demands, the sudden dropping of a case, or the failure of an agency to reply. These are wins, even if not reported.

Examples of honourable paperwork exist throughout history. Merchants once settled disputes across continents using notices and affidavits. Without modern courts, they relied on written truth and timelines. If no rebuttal came, the matter was settled. The same principles apply today. Commerce has not changed. The Crown corporation itself relies on them. Sovereigns simply use the same tools to expose deception. When applied with honour, they are impossible to defeat.

The lesson of notices, affidavits, and conditional acceptance is simple yet profound. The system survives by presumption. It assumes consent because men and women remain silent. The remedy is to speak truth on the record. A notice declares it. An affidavit swears it. Conditional acceptance demands proof. Together, they dismantle presumption and reclaim sovereignty. They show that a living man or woman is greater than any corporate entity.

In Canada, where statutes and courts appear overwhelming, these tools return power to the individual. They prove that you are not powerless. You do not need lawyers or politicians to defend you. You hold the greatest power already: your word, your honour, your truth. When placed on the record properly, it stands higher than any statute. The Crown cannot rebut life. It can only deceive. Notices, affidavits, and conditional acceptance strip away the deception and reveal truth.

The sovereign man or woman who masters these tools no longer fears government letters, court summonses, or bank demands. They respond calmly, in writing, with honour. They demand proof, accept conditionally, and place facts on record. They do not argue. They do not rebel. They stand. In doing so, they expose the fraud and reclaim freedom. Paperwork, simple as it may seem, becomes the sword and shield of sovereignty.

# Chapter 12: Standing in Honour as a Living Canadian

Knowledge without action is powerless. Understanding the Strawman, the Crown corporation, the Charter illusion, taxation by consent, licences, Admiralty courts, policy enforcers, banking fraud, programming in schools, and media manipulation is only the first step. The true test of sovereignty is living by it. To be a sovereign man or woman in Canada is not to argue endlessly or to fight angrily. It is to stand in honour, in every interaction, every word, and every action. Honour is the foundation of freedom. Without it, sovereignty collapses into rebellion or chaos. With it, sovereignty shines as truth.

Honour means you do not break your word. It means you do not cause harm, you do not commit fraud, and you keep your agreements. This is natural law, the only law that binds the living. All else is policy. When you live by honour, you rise above statutes and codes. You cannot be controlled, because you give no cause for claims. The Crown corporation depends on dishonour: silence, fear, aggression, or fraud. It struggles when faced with men and women who live truthfully and act with integrity. Honour is its weakness, and your greatest strength.

Standing in honour begins with language. The words you use define your position. When asked if you are a citizen, taxpayer, or resident, the sovereign replies calmly: "I am a living man." When addressed by the Strawman name, the sovereign asks, "Who is being addressed." When asked to understand, the sovereign replies, "I do not stand under jurisdiction." These are not arguments. They are statements of truth. Honour requires you to speak clearly, without deception. Never lie, never evade, never misrepresent. Truth is your shield.

Paperwork, as explained in the previous chapter, is a tool of honour. A notice declares truth. An affidavit swears it. Conditional acceptance shows willingness with conditions. These are honourable acts, because they do not refuse blindly or lash out. They accept in principle but require proof. Honour does not mean submission. It means calm strength. It is saying: I will comply if you prove lawful authority. If you cannot, I cannot agree. Honour leaves no room for accusation. It disarms the system, which expects hostility.

Living in honour also means taking responsibility. The sovereign does not rely on government for welfare, licences, or benefits. To accept such benefits is to enter contract. To refuse them is to stand free. This requires courage. It may mean building your own livelihood, teaching your own children, or relying on community rather than the state. Honour means living consistently with your principles. If you declare sovereignty but still seek government benefits, you contradict yourself. Honour requires sacrifice, but it rewards with freedom.

Encounters with police are tests of honour. Officers expect fear or aggression. They are trained to exploit dishonour. The sovereign remains calm. He does not argue, insult, or resist violently. He asks questions: "Am I obliged to comply. Under what authority. Where is the contract." He identifies as a living man, not a driver, citizen, or taxpayer. He does not consent silently. He does not create joinder. If threatened, he remains calm, standing on truth. Honour frightens officers because they cannot counter it. They rely on intimidation, but intimidation fails against calm truth.

Honour in courts is equally vital. Judges expect pleas, arguments, and submissions. The sovereign gives none. He states truth on the record: "I am a living man. I do not consent to joinder. Where is the contract binding me." He submits notices and affidavits, calmly and clearly. He does not insult the judge or shout. He does not rebel. He stands in honour, refusing to be treated as cargo in Admiralty commerce. Courts struggle with this, because honour cannot be dismissed. Judges may threaten or mock, but they cannot rebut truth. Honour is stronger than robes.

Honour also applies to daily life. The sovereign pays debts voluntarily agreed, keeps promises, and treats others fairly. He does not exploit loopholes or cheat neighbours. Sovereignty is not an excuse for selfishness. It is responsibility lived openly. The man who harms others or breaks agreements dishonours himself, and his claim to sovereignty collapses. The corporation thrives on dishonour, because dishonour creates claims. Honour removes claims, leaving nothing for the system to exploit.

Community is strengthened by honour. When sovereign men and women gather, they build trust by living truthfully. They trade fairly, teach openly, and support one another. They do not need contracts, because honour is enough. This terrifies the Crown corporation, because it cannot control communities that live in truth. It can only control individuals bound by fear, debt, and dishonour. Communities built on honour stand outside its reach, free and sovereign.

Standing in honour requires courage. The system will mock, threaten, and sometimes punish. Friends and family may not understand. The path is lonely at times. Yet honour sustains. It provides strength no statute can break. A man who knows he has caused no harm, committed no fraud, and broken no agreements cannot be enslaved. He may be pressured, but he remains free in spirit. Honour is the foundation of sovereignty because it cannot be taken away. It is the highest law, written not on paper but in life itself.

Standing in honour also means refusing to act in anger. The system thrives on confrontation. When a man shouts at police or insults a judge, he creates dishonour. Courts then treat him as hostile, justifying penalties. The sovereign avoids this trap. He speaks calmly, asks questions, and places truth on the record. He does not fight with emotion. He stands with reason. This approach disarms the corporation, which is prepared for rebellion but powerless against calm honour.

Living as a sovereign in Canada demands that one recognise contracts at every step. Every licence, tax return, and government form is an invitation to consent. Honour requires that you examine these offers carefully. If you choose to accept, do so knowingly. If you choose to decline, do so with respect and clarity. Conditional acceptance is a form of honour, because it shows willingness if lawful proof exists. Dishonour would be to refuse blindly, or to accept while secretly rejecting. Honour requires transparency.

Spiritual strength is also part of honour. Many sovereign men and women recognise that they are not simply bodies or names, but living souls. They draw courage from this truth. Courts and corporations cannot touch the soul. They can only address the Strawman. Honour means remembering that you are more than paper. This perspective brings peace even in confrontation. A man who knows he is life itself does not fear threats to his Strawman. He stands in honour, unshaken by the illusions of power.

Practical habits support this way of living. Keep clear records of your notices, affidavits, and communications. Date every document, make copies, and store them safely. Honour requires clarity, and clarity requires evidence. If ever challenged, you can show the record of your truth. The corporation relies on confusion. By keeping order, you remain strong. Sovereigns who live with discipline in paperwork and conduct protect themselves from dishonour.

Honour also requires humility. Sovereignty is not about domination or superiority. It is not about proving others wrong or boasting of victories. It is about living truthfully, quietly, and consistently. The man who flaunts sovereignty risks pride, which leads to dishonour. The man who lives humbly in honour inspires others without words. Sovereignty spreads not through arguments but through example. When neighbours see a life lived peacefully and freely, they are encouraged to follow.

Challenges will arise. Employers demand Social Insurance Numbers. Banks demand identification. Police demand licences. Courts demand pleas. Each challenge is an invitation to dishonour. Honour means responding calmly, refusing joinder, and asking for proof. You may not always win in appearance. The court may threaten, the officer may fine, the bank may close an account. Yet if you remain consistent, you remain sovereign. True victory is not in escaping every inconvenience. It is in living truth regardless of circumstance.

The power of honour is cumulative. Each time you respond with truth, you strengthen your standing. Each notice filed, each affidavit unrebutted, each conditional acceptance unanswered builds a record of sovereignty. Over time, the system learns to leave sovereign men and women alone, because they are too difficult to trap. The corporation prefers easy prey—those who comply without question. Honourable men and women are obstacles it would rather avoid.

Honour also has a higher purpose. It reconnects men and women to each other. In a society ruled by contracts and statutes, trust is eroded. Neighbours sue neighbours, families fight over wills, and strangers fear one another. Sovereigns rebuild trust by living honourably. They show that agreements can be kept without contracts, that peace can exist without police, that justice can prevail without courts. This way of life inspires communities to reclaim independence from the Crown.

The path of honour is not easy, but it is simple. Speak truth, cause no harm, commit no fraud, honour agreements. Refuse contracts that compromise your sovereignty. Stand calmly against threats. Live consistently with your principles. These steps do not require wealth, status, or education. They require only courage and integrity. Every Canadian has the power to live this way. The only obstacle is fear.

When fear fades, sovereignty flourishes. A man who no longer fears ridicule, fines, or threats cannot be controlled. He is free in spirit, even if the corporation harasses him. Honour gives this freedom. It makes the sovereign untouchable where it matters most—in truth. Governments may seize property, banks may freeze accounts, courts may issue threats, but honour remains beyond their reach. It is the true fortress of sovereignty, stronger than any statute, deeper than any deception.

Standing in honour as a living Canadian is the final step on the path. Knowledge opens the door, but honour walks through it. Without honour, sovereignty is empty talk. With honour, it is life itself. The man or woman who lives this way is not subject, not citizen, not taxpayer. They are free. They stand as proof that the Crown corporation does not own life. They remind all who see them that freedom is not granted. It is lived.

# Conclusion: The Path Forward in Canada

The path of sovereignty is not theory. It is not debate, nor is it rebellion. It is the quiet and steady act of living as a free man or woman. Canada is a land of beauty and abundance, yet its people are bound by illusions—illusions of government, of citizenship, of law, of money, of media. These illusions are strong only because they are believed. Once exposed, they lose power. The path forward is simple: stop consenting to deception and start living in honour.

The first step is knowledge. Without knowledge, sovereignty is impossible. Canadians must understand the Strawman and how it was created at birth. They must recognise Canada as a Crown corporation, not a free nation. They must see the Charter as a licence, not a shield. They must realise that taxation is by consent, that licences are contracts, that courts operate in Admiralty commerce, that police are policy enforcers, that banks create money from nothing, that schools program obedience, and that media shapes perception. This knowledge strips away illusions and reveals truth.

The second step is action. Knowledge without action leaves you trapped. Action does not mean violence or protest. It means living as a sovereign. It means refusing joinder, asking for proof, and standing calmly in honour. It means issuing notices and affidavits, conditionally accepting demands, and keeping records. It means living without fear, knowing that the Crown corporation has no lawful authority over life. Action is where theory becomes freedom.

The third step is community. Sovereignty is not isolation. A man or woman alone can resist, but communities built on honour thrive. Families, neighbours, and friends who trade fairly, teach truth, and support one another weaken the corporation's grip. The Crown thrives on division—citizen against citizen, group against group, neighbour against neighbour. Sovereignty thrives on unity. Communities of honour show that people can govern themselves without corporate control. They are living proof that freedom works.

The path forward also requires courage. The system will not yield easily. Courts will mock, police will threaten, banks will resist, and media will ridicule. Friends may doubt, family may worry. Yet honour gives strength. A man who knows he is free cannot be enslaved by ridicule. A woman who knows she is sovereign cannot be intimidated by threats. Courage is not the absence of fear. It is standing in truth despite fear. Each act of courage weakens the system and strengthens sovereignty.

Canadians must also reclaim responsibility. Sovereignty is not licence to act without consequence. It is the highest form of responsibility. To live free is to live with integrity. To provide for family without welfare, to trade without cheating, to honour agreements without courts, to resolve disputes without violence—these are the marks of sovereignty. Responsibility is freedom's twin. Without it, freedom degenerates into chaos. With it, freedom becomes life.

The role of paperwork will remain central. Notices, affidavits, and conditional acceptance are the language of commerce. They place truth on the record and expose presumption. Sovereigns must master this language. It is not complicated, but it requires discipline. Write clearly. Speak truthfully. Keep timelines. Stand firm. The Crown cannot withstand honour on the record. Its silence is admission. Its failure to respond is agreement. Paperwork is the sword and shield of the free.

The path forward will not be the same for everyone. Some may choose to challenge taxes. Others may refuse licences. Some may withdraw children from schools. Others may focus on building local communities. Each act weakens the Crown and strengthens sovereignty. There is no single strategy. The key is to live consistently with truth. Whatever steps you take, take them in honour. Never lie, never cheat, never harm. Stand calmly, and freedom follows.

In time, more Canadians will awaken. Illusions cannot last forever. The cracks are already visible: debt levels unsustainable, trust in government collapsing, media credibility eroding. Each failure of the system reveals its fraud. When enough men and women see through the illusion, the Crown corporation will lose its hold. A nation of sovereigns cannot be ruled by deception. It can only be served by honour. The future belongs not to corporations but to living people who remember who they are.

The path forward is not easy, but it is simple. Live truth. Refuse deception. Stand in honour. Support one another. This is the way to reclaim freedom in Canada. The Crown will resist, but it cannot win against life itself. You were born free. No paper, no statute, no charter, no licence, no contract can change that. The system survives only when you forget. The path forward is to remember.

The future of sovereignty in Canada rests on choice. Each man and woman must decide whether to live as a subject or as a sovereign. The subject accepts illusions, signs contracts without thought, obeys statutes without question, and hopes the Crown will be merciful. The sovereign accepts responsibility, refuses deception, and lives in honour. The difference is profound, yet the choice is simple. Freedom is not granted. It is lived.

The system has lasted this long because most Canadians have chosen comfort over truth. They trade sovereignty for convenience, believing licences protect them, taxes support them, schools educate them, and media inform them. They avoid ridicule by conforming. They avoid conflict by complying. Yet this comfort is fading. Debt rises, freedoms shrink, and trust in government declines. The cost of submission grows heavier each year. The moment is coming when Canadians must decide whether to continue as subjects or rise as sovereigns.

The strength of the system is its illusions. It hides behind robes, badges, paperwork, and screens. It intimidates with threats and ridicules with mockery. But illusions are fragile. They dissolve when faced with truth. A judge who cannot produce a contract, a police officer who cannot prove obligation, a tax agency that cannot rebut an affidavit—these moments reveal the weakness of the Crown. Sovereigns who stand in honour expose these cracks. Each crack widens until the illusion collapses.

The strength of sovereignty is honour. A man who keeps his word cannot be controlled. A woman who causes no harm cannot be punished. A community that trades fairly cannot be enslaved. Honour disarms deception. It makes every statute unnecessary and every threat powerless. Honour is the path forward because it cannot be taken away. It exists within each man and woman, waiting to be lived.

The journey will not be the same for all. Some will awaken slowly, questioning media narratives. Others will begin by resisting taxes or refusing licences. Some will teach their children outside the system. Others will focus on community trade and mutual support. Each step matters. Each act of sovereignty chips away at the corporation. The path forward is not about uniformity. It is about living truth in your own life, and inspiring others by example.

Courage is the bridge between knowledge and action. Many know the system is corrupt, yet they fear standing against it. They fear ridicule, fines, or inconvenience. Sovereignty requires stepping beyond that fear. Courage grows with practice. Each time you issue a notice, each time you refuse joinder, each time you stand calmly against intimidation, courage deepens. Over time, fear fades. Honour replaces it. This is how sovereignty spreads: one courageous act at a time.

The Crown corporation cannot withstand a nation of sovereigns. It survives only by presumption. If millions withdraw consent, it has no power. Police cannot enforce statutes against all. Courts cannot process everyone. Banks cannot profit from those who refuse fraudulent contracts. The corporation collapses when consent is withdrawn. That collapse need not be violent. It can be peaceful, gradual, and honourable. Sovereigns build new systems of trade, education, and justice while the old system withers.

The role of community in this future cannot be overstated. Sovereignty thrives when men and women support each other. A man who grows food can share with a neighbour who builds. A teacher of natural law can guide children while others provide shelter. Together, they form communities that function without government. These communities already exist in small ways across Canada. They are seeds of freedom. The path forward is to nurture them, expand them, and connect them.

The final lesson is personal responsibility. Freedom is not about doing whatever you please. It is about living truthfully and accepting the consequences of your choices. A sovereign who harms others loses honour. A sovereign who breaks agreements destroys credibility. The path forward requires discipline. Speak carefully, act responsibly, and live consistently. Sovereignty is not selfishness. It is service to life, to truth, and to community.

This book has laid out the path: from the creation of the Strawman to the deception of the Crown corporation, from the Charter illusion to taxation by consent, from licences and Admiralty courts to police enforcers, banks, schools, and media. Each chapter exposed a chain. Each chain can be broken. The key is knowledge, honour, and courage. Together, they form the path forward.

The message is simple: you are not property. You are not a citizen, taxpayer, or debtor. You are a living man or woman, born free. The Crown corporation survives only when you forget this truth. The path forward is to remember, to live it, and to share it. When enough Canadians do, freedom will no longer be theory. It will be life.

The path is open. The choice is yours.

## Don't miss out!

Visit the website below and you can sign up to receive emails whenever Roger Davies publishes a new book. There's no charge and no obligation.

https://books2read.com/r/B-A-HHGNE-SJAYG

BOOKS 2 READ

Connecting independent readers to independent writers.

Did you love *Standing as a Living Man or Woman in Canada: Reclaiming Freedom Beyond Statutes and Policy*? Then you should read *Freedom by Rebuttal: How to Say No and Stand Free*[1] by Roger Davies!

[2]

Freedom is not a gift from Parliament, courts, or officials. It is your birthright. Yet nearly every man and woman lives under taxes, debts, licences, and endless demands. The system does not force you with chains. It binds you with silence.

Freedom by Rebuttal shows how silence is turned into consent — and how you can take that consent back. This book is a practical guide to saying no lawfully, standing in honour, and using words instead of anger to collapse false claims.

Roger Davies takes you through the principles and practices of rebuttal step by step:

---

1. https://books2read.com/u/bxpM1v

2. https://books2read.com/u/bxpM1v

• How silence is treated as agreement in law• The Strawman trap and how to separate from it• Why honour is essential and how to keep it• The power of conditional acceptance: "Yes, on proof of claim"• Writing notices that shift the burden of proof back to the claimant• Turning notices into affidavits that stand as truth when unrebutted• Using rebuttal against council tax, banking debts, and fines• Responding to police and court summons with calm questions• Building community strength and supporting others who rebut

This is not a book of magic words or quick fixes. It does not promise that you will never face pressure. It shows you how to remain calm, how to act in honour, and how to put the other party on the record. When you rebut a claim with lawful notice, you remove presumption. When you conditionally accept on proof, you force the claimant to prove authority — and they usually cannot.

Freedom by Rebuttal explains that courts, councils, and banks rely on dishonour and silence to gain power. They thrive when you argue in anger or remain quiet in fear. Honourable rebuttal defeats both traps. It leaves you standing as a living man or woman, not a corporate fiction.

You will learn how to draft notices and affidavits, how to keep proper records, and how to respond when officials ignore your requests. You will see real examples of men and women who used rebuttal to collapse council tax cases, challenge false debts, and end claims in court.

This book is written for those who sense that something is wrong but are not sure what to do next. It offers practical tools that can be used daily — when a letter arrives, when a demand is made, or when you are called into court.

Freedom by Rebuttal is not rebellion. It is remedy. It is about placing your truth on the record, giving lawful notice, and refusing to be bound without contract. It is about taking back consent peacefully, with calm strength and patience.

If you are ready to stop living in silent agreement, if you are ready to face the system without fear, this book will show you how. The first step is simple: say no, and stand free.

# Also by Roger Davies

**Sovereign Foundations: Liberty, Rights, Consent**

The Constitution of One: How the Bill of Rights Protects the Sovereign Man & Woman

From Subjects to Sovereigns: Reclaiming the Spirit of 1776

Liberty by Consent: Reclaiming Freedom Through the Law of Consent

**Standalone**

The Commonwealth Corporation: How Australia Was Turned Into a Business

The Legal Fiction: The Greatest Trick Ever Played on Humanity

The Sovereign Path: Living Free Beyond the System

Common Law: The True Law of the Living

Freedom by Rebuttal: How to Say No and Stand Free

The Magna Carta: Why It Is Important to Sovereign Men and Women

The Trust Game: Hidden Estates and the Cestui Que Vie Act

Freedom by Notice: Winning with Paperwork

The Hidden Contracts: How Governments Enslave the People

The Law of the Living: Admiralty Shadows and the Path to Sovereignty

Standing as a Living Man or Woman in Canada: Reclaiming Freedom Beyond Statutes and Policy

# About the Author

Roger Davies researches the crossroads of commerce, policy, and personal sovereignty. He writes for readers who sense there is more to the story, who are ready to replace fear with honour and paperwork with plain truth. When not writing, he helps men and women organise their records, challenge unfounded claims, and build communities grounded in mutual aid and responsibility.